FREE

FREELY GIVEN

The Story of Scripture Gift Mission

by

Phyllis Thompson

HODDER AND STOUGHTON
LONDON SYDNEY AUCKLAND TORONTO

British Library Cataloguing in Publication Data

Thompson, Phyllis, *1906–*
   Freely given : the story of the Scripture
   Gift Mission.
   1. Scripture Gift Mission—History
   I. Title
   266′.023   BV2370.S3

ISBN 0 340 41587 8

Hodder and Stoughton Editorial Office: 47 Bedford Square, London WC1B 3DP

Contents

Foreword

by Professor Donald Wiseman
Chairman of Scripture Gift Mission Council

It was in the dark days of World War II that my personal interest in Scripture Gift Mission (SGM) began. Following an Air Ministry conference there were only two days left in London to try to find Bibles in Italian for which the Christians in newly liberated southern Italy were pleading. I thought of SGM, for as a serving officer I had received a crested New Testament which I carried with me and in it was the address of the Mission at Radstock House in Eccleston Street near Victoria. I went there for help and the Secretary, Mr Ashley Baker, said we must pray about it. When we rose from kneeling on the rather hard stained boards of the old building he smiled and said, 'Our God always answers prayer.' However, first he made me promise to take a small parcel to the Belgian Gospel Mission at Brussels on my way back to Naples. In the event it weighed nearly a ton! The next morning my Dakota took off from Hendon with every spare cargo space crammed with boxes of Bibles and Scripture handbooks. The crew handled them aboard willingly – at first – thinking they contained food and beer!

A mission that can seize the opportunity of a passing moment to help individuals and churches worldwide, without question of cost and labour, was the one for my support – as it has been ever since. *Freely Given* tells the faithbuilding story of how throughout the years the Lord God has never failed to provide the means, and how the Mission has remained as flexible as ever in providing the printed Word where it is needed.

Personal evangelism and Christian teaching to make the Good News of Jesus Christ and life in God known and lived out is as much needed today as it was a hundred years ago when SGM was founded. This book tells something of the Mission's aims and activities. It is not a history. It is an inside, as well as an outside, view of some of the ways God has enabled the Mission to serve others by providing, without charge, portions of Scripture in more than 750 different languages to be freely given in personal evangelism. The book shows the way that the Word of God, often in selections of Scripture chosen for a given situation, is passed on with prayer, personal commendation and witness, and with practical encouragement in a variety of situations the world over. Blessing has followed as the Word passes to people in home, hospital, church, school or college, in busy market-place or lonely solitude, in war and peace.

Phyllis Thompson uses her missionary experience and the skilful pen of a ready writer to give a vivid picture drawn from many facets. Nevertheless, the work of many individuals, committee and staff members and the host of distributors, has to be left unspoken.

The Lord announced the Word and great was the company of those who proclaimed it (Psalm 68:11).

It is our prayer that this book will move the reader to pray for others and also help them hand on the Word of Life in every possible way. May it also bring praise to God as the great initiator, sustainer and encourager of all His works and workers.

Donald Wiseman

1

Disaster Unannounced

No one paid any attention to the two gas men who had arrived in the vicinity of Eccleston Street, Belgravia, that Monday afternoon in April, 1956. They were merely engaged in a routine job of checking pipes. Pedestrians had to step aside at the place on the pavement where they were working, but the traffic continued up and down the busy roads unimpeded.

Everything appeared quite normal. There was nothing to give any indication that a major disaster was about to take place.

The reporters in the BBC Television Unit that was cruising towards Victoria Station were completely unaware that one of the most spectacular news scoops they would ever encounter unannounced was awaiting them. As for the staff and employees of Scripture Gift Mission, situated in the tall Victorian building on the corner of Eccleston Street and Eccleston Place, they were all even busier than usual, for they had been away at their annual weekend conference together, and not having arrived at work until 11 a.m. were trying to make up for lost time.

It had been an enjoyable weekend for them all, with wives joining them, as well as a number of Council members. Once again it had served to cement the family spirit among them, and the consciousness of fellowship and purpose in a work that confined most of them to the mundane environment of office and warehouse. The keeping of records, the typing of letters, the packing of parcels might become monotonous, but what they were doing was affecting their fellow creatures all over the world. The Scripture Gift Mission (SGM) emphasis was essentially individual rather than collective, and to be working there was not unlike being in a sort of spiritual dispensary, where pills and capsules, oils and vitamins, all had to be tabulated, sorted and despatched according to prescription.

The leaflets and booklets, New Testaments and Bibles that were sent off, free of charge, to people scattered throughout the five continents who would put them to good use, were carefully prepared and chosen to meet specific requirements.

Four Things God Wants you to Know for the careless, *Daily Strength* for the weary, *The Way of Salvation* for the seeker, and so on, could meet human needs the world over. And from time to time news came that it was happening...

'A friend of mine, who up to a little while ago was an atheist, was soundly converted through a personal chat and through studying your booklet *Old and New Life*.'

A semi-literate Peruvian man from a remote village in the Andes bought a New Testament in his own language and took it home. Two years later, as the result of reading aloud from it every evening, practically everyone in the village had come to Christ.

The leader of a small party on a scientific expedition to the borders of the Arctic, who had all received a copy of *Daily Strength* which they read together each day wrote:

'All of us experienced the presence of the Holy Spirit in a wonderful way. I could not begin to tell you of the way God led us, guided us. It was a vivid and very wonderful experience.'

A missionary in the Middle East travelling on a crowded bus one day, gave the Arabic leaflet *Eternal Life* to a fellow passenger. 'He readily received it, and said he wanted a book about Jesus Christ. When we got off the bus, he waited whilst

I went and fetched the Gospels of Luke and John in Arabic. I saw him again the other day. He said he had questions to ask, and wanted to come along one evening for a chat.'

These extracts were usually read out at the fifteen-minute staff prayer meetings held each day at 9 a.m. and 2 p.m., and since all had lent a hand, however remotely, in getting the literature off, they went back to their jobs stimulated with a sense of fulfilment. They were in it together. The annual conference was the culminating event in the programme, aimed at refreshing and encouraging the whole team, and this year's weekend had been no exception.

Everything had gone well, if uneventfully. The only thing that had been rather surprising was at the Sunday morning service, when the speaker told them that being awakened in the night, he did not know why, he felt compelled to change the talk he had prepared and speak, instead, on the words, 'Fear Not'. He mentioned that the phrase was found fifty-three times in Scripture, one for every week, 'and an extra one because you never know when you will need it!'

'Fear not.' The message seemed rather irrelevant in their peaceful, congenial surroundings, and had not really made a great impression at the time. The weekend had passed happily, with much chatting together at tables where meals were spread they had not had to prepare, and from which they rose without having to do any washing up. Instead, they could go for strolls in the grounds before gathering to sing and pray and listen to Bible expositions. They felt the better for it, and now it was back to work, suitcases containing their best clothes stacked in the cloakrooms.

The times of the tea breaks had been altered, so the first lot of workers had already passed to the kitchen through the showroom, leaving it empty but for the receptionist, and someone from the Translations Department who was chatting to a visitor.

Out in the street the two gas men had opened a rusty cockstop, and were trying to close it again.

Up in the Secretary's office on the first floor, Ashley Baker
was behind his desk, Winifred Marden beside him with her
notebook, Mighell Smith and Archie Long, with representatives from Scotland and Ireland sitting facing them. They
were discussing the need for the work to become more widely
known, when one after another they sniffed, looked at each
other and said simultaneously,

'It smells like gas . . .'

On the floor above Ken Andrewartha was sitting at his roll-
top desk in the Translations Department, studying the
manuscript that had just arrived. It was two feet long by one
foot wide, eight Bible stories translated into Malay Jawi
script, which had been carefully written ten times the usual
size, according to instructions, by an elderly missionary
working on the border of south Thailand and Malaysia.

He had made a good job of it, Ken decided as he cast his
practised eye over it. The hieroglyphics would be perfectly
clear when the whole thing was reduced to size, and if things
could be speeded up, a couple of thousand copies, containing
their message of salvation, could be on their way for
distribution among Muslims within two months.

That elderly missionary G. K. Harris deserved all the help
he could get. He had spent a lifetime among Muslims in
China, and when that country closed to missionaries he was
due for retirement. But he hadn't retired. There were Muslims
who knew nothing about the living Christ in other parts of
Asia, so to them he had gone.

He was an enterprising man. He lived just over the border
from Malaysia, where Christian missionary work among
Muslims was forbidden, so he did not put his head in that
noose by trying to do it. Instead, he got on the trains as they
came over the border into South Thailand, where there was
no law to stop him evangelising whoever would listen to him.
The Muslim traders on those trains became quite accustomed
to seeing a tallish, elderly white man walking up and down in
the corridors, a satchel over his shoulder from which he

would extract an interestingly illustrated leaflet and give it to anyone he had had a chat with. If the recipient saw with surprise that it was written in his own language, and if he took it home with him back over the border into Malaysia, so much the better. No law had been broken, and yet a little portion of the Word of God had got into a land closed against it.

Literature, like thistledown, floats over all sorts of barriers, finds its way into the remotest of places, and when there is life in it, it can take root and blossom wherever there is soil to receive it.

G. K. Harris, in his itinerations, had come across a group of people into whose particular dialect no portion of the Word of God had been translated, so now he wanted an SGM leaflet to distribute among them. These Bible stories would make a good beginning, and Ken was ready to do everything in his power to provide him with them.

Correspondence about it had been going on for months, culminating in the arrival of this carefully prepared manuscript. It represented many hours of concentrated labour, and Ken was absorbed in studying it when his nose wrinkled, and he muttered,

'Whew! What a smell! Creosote – must be painters about', and returned to the manuscript.

The two gas men out in the street were looking at each other rather anxiously.

'Better go and find out where this pipe leads to,' said one of them, and springing up from the hole in the pavement hurried into the side door of the building.

Simultaneously Ronald Young, his desk covered with correspondence from the Middle East, opened the door of his office and started running down the stairs calling,

'Joe! Joe! Where's that gas coming from?' Another door opened and a female voice cried,

'Joe! Joe! There's a smell of gas...'

Joe, lithe and agile, was bounding up from the basement

when the gas man inside the door saw him and asked urgently,

'Where does your gas pipe lead to!'

With a jerk of the head Joe turned and ran ahead of him back down the stairs into the basement. He had just reached the five foot high wall that separated the boiler from the rest of the area when it happened.

A blinding flash.

A deafening roar.

Masonry crumbling. Paving stones flung into the air. Slates flying off the roof. Windows shattered.

Then there were flames.

The biggest explosion in London since the Second World War had taken place, in the Scripture Gift Mission, and nobody knew what had happened.

The Post Office clock on the opposite side of the road had stopped. The time was 3.33 p.m.

Ken Andrewartha, hearing the explosion and conscious that files were flying and furniture toppling over, as in an air raid, instinctively plunged under his desk.

Mighell Smith, his hand on the door he had just opened, felt himself gently but firmly lifted off his feet and deposited in a heap halfway across the Secretary's room. Winifred Marden dropped her notebook and put her hands to her head to shield it from falling furniture. Ashley Baker tried to get out of his chair, but found himself wedged. Archie Long wondered what had hit him on the head.

Ronald Young, hurrying along the passage found himself flattened against the wall, vision blurred and breathless. Packers in the store rooms started groping their way over bundles of booklets that were bouncing off the shelves. Girls in the offices screamed as flying glass and crumbling plaster showered over them, and steel filing cabinets toppled over. 'Joe! Joe! Where's Joe?'

But Joe was lying unconscious on a pile of rubble on the floor of the boiler room.

*

Sirens sounded shrilly as police cars, fire engines, ambulances all converged on Eccleston Street. The area was cordoned off, and traffic diverted, while onlookers stood in groups looking with horror at the building that was going up in flames on the corner of Eccleston Place.

The garage men in the car hire firm opposite were feverishly squirting spray foam on the petrol pumps, uneasily aware that under their feet was a 3,000 gallon tank. The spraying over, they leaped into the cars with shattered windscreens and dented bodies (Rolls Royces among them) and drove them out before more damage was done.

An amateur photographer, with great presence of mind, rushed to the top of his building, held his camera firmly, focussed carefully, and took the picture that was to appear, to his delight, in a prominent position in his favourite newspaper the very next morning.

The BBC Television men were up on the roof of the nearest high building, giving live coverage to the fire that became headline news throughout the country.

Taxis carrying reporters eager to get to the scene as quickly as possible were speeding towards Victoria, and another taxi, too, carrying a passenger who was more concerned than any of them to find out what was happening. The Chairman of Scripture Gift Mission, Frank Henman, had received an urgent phone call in his office in the City, and jumping up from his desk had left everything to get to the scene of the disaster as soon as he could.

Scripture Gift Mission, metaphorically speaking, was his life. When a young man, he had hoped to go to China as a missionary, but his medical report was against him, so he said, 'All right, Lord. My health may be bad, but I'm good at business, so I'll use the gifts I have, make money and use it for You!'

Reinforced concrete was what eventually made him financially, and he was as good as his word when it came to using his money. The life style he and his family adopted was as modest as that of many of his employees. But he wanted to use more than his money. He wanted to devote himself as a person to do service for the extension of the Kingdom of God, and decided he could best do that by directing his energies in one channel. His money might go in various directions, but only one could absorb him, his intellect, his concern, his mental activity.

Scripture Gift Mission was that one, and those who knew the organisation said that Frank Henman had not only reinforced concrete, but had reinforced SGM as well.

When he arrived at Eccleston Street he found Ashley Baker in the London City Mission House opposite, anxiously going round the groups of men and women, some with faces blackened and clothes singed, who had staggered across the road from the burning building into the haven so readily opened to them. Were all the members of his staff accounted for? The translations assistant in the showroom had been seriously injured, and taken off to hospital in an ambulance. Some of the others were badly shaken, almost in a state of shock. Those on the same floor as Ken Andrewartha had been imprisoned behind doors that were jammed with fallen furniture until Ken and some of the other men had released them, and by that time flames were rising, and they looked down on gaping holes in the floor where the boards had been blown out. But there was a sort of zigzag path of cross-beams along which they walked, one by one, all holding hands, until they got to the stone stairs, and made their escape.

There had been no sign of Joe in all the activity of evacuating the premises until Mighell Smith, going in again through the side door of the blazing building, saw a slowly crawling figure dragging an inert form along the floor.

'Joe!' he cried, and hurried forward.

Joe's face was black and his hair half burnt off, but he managed to gasp, 'It's the gas man... found him on the ground...'

Joe had recovered consciousness largely because of the

acute pain on his scalp. His hair was scorched, flames licking around him, and he had become dimly aware of distant sounds of sirens and shouting. He beat out the flames on his head, but it hurt to do it, and desperately he looked around. Everything was in darkness until he discerned, beyond the outlines of shelves and cupboards leaning crazily at all angles, a faint glimmer of daylight. He started crawling towards it, clambering over or around piles of rubble and wood and iron girders until he came upon something that was soft and yielding. Peering down, he saw it was the figure of the gas man, his face covered in blood, arm crumpled under him. There was nothing else for it but to get him out, too, dragging him along...

All told, Joe was very glad to see Mighell Smith, and very relieved to be helped into the ambulance and whisked off to hospital. The gas man was taken too, of course, and other members of staff. But as Ashley Baker went over the men and women who worked with him and whom he knew so well, he found that they were all accounted for, and all alive.

'Thank God!' he said fervently. Then he added, 'Now we know why we had that message on Sunday morning. "Fear not! Fear not!"' And as some of them sat around, thankfully drinking the tea the London City Mission was providing, they recounted the significant happenings that had prevented things from being so very, very much worse than they were.

'If it hadn't been for the changed time of the tea break, most of us would have been passing through the showroom to and from the kitchen at the very time of the explosion,' said Winifred Marden. The showroom had taken the worst of the blast, being directly above the boiler. 'I wonder how many of us would have been here now, if it hadn't been for that change of time!'

'That side door had been blocked for days with bundles of literature,' observed someone else. 'They were only moved late on Friday afternoon. They might have been left there till

today. What if we hadn't been able to get out of that
door...!'

'The stocks, too!' They looked ruefully at the bundles of
Scriptures, scorched by fire and sodden with water, that the
men were bringing across the street in their efforts to salvage
something. 'What a good thing so much of it had been taken
to the warehouse at Clapham before this happened!'

So they had an impromptu thanksgiving service on the
spot, out of gratitude for their deliverance. The reporters who
were writing rapidly in their notebooks were mystified. They
did not know quite what to make of it. The consternation of
the garage men in the car hire firm at the damage done to the
Rolls Royces they could understand, but to be praying and
thanking God in such circumstances was sufficiently unusual
to make them take note. At any rate, it came into the category
known as "News". The editors would make something of it.

GIRLS PRAY AS FLAMES DESTROY BIBLE BUILDING was the
headline blazoned across the top of a popular daily the
following morning, while another entitled its report, 50 FLEE
FIRE, THEN GIVE THANKS WITH PRAYER.

Reports in the evening papers the same day were not so
full. The reporters only had time to find out where the fire was
raging, get some impressions from bystanders as to what had
happened – 'Three bad rumbles, then a big cloud of smoke
and flames forty to fifty feet high', '... heard a terrific
explosion, rushed out, heard a woman screaming in the
basement, helped her out...' – and tear off to the nearest
telephone with their reports.

Their information, if scanty, made good headlines, and
shared the honours on the front pages with Khrushchev's
boast that Russia had the lead with the H-bomb and with
pictures of Prince Rainier and Princess Grace of Monaco on
their honeymoon. By the time SGM workers had brushed off
as much as they could of the plaster and splintered glass that
had showered upon them, straightened their clothes, sponged
their faces, and set off rather shakily for the buses and

underground trains that would take them home, the papers were on the news stands, and large size posters were announcing a great London explosion. SGM workers found themselves in the news. Most of them had only the clothes, some singed, all smelling of smoke, they stood up in. Their purses, bags and suitcases were all gone.

But they did not set off for home empty-handed. It was typical of Frank Henman that he thought of the practical things, and sent off Ashley Baker post haste to their bank. It was already closed, but opened for the emergency, so that he could draw out fifty ten-shilling notes to be distributed all round. At least they would have enough for their fares, and some over. They must have felt rather like those who shared the shipwreck with the apostle Paul, of whom it is reported that they all escaped safe to land.*

As one who was in it reflected thirty years later, 'It was a deep spiritual experience for those involved, an enriching occasion for deeper fellowship and self-forgetfulness, and a revelation in retrospect of widespread Christian affection.'

At the time, however, it looked like a disaster sufficiently overwhelming as to threaten the very existence of the Mission.

So it seemed to Norman Brown of the Liverpool office when he heard about it the following day. He was in Switzerland at the time, acting as padre in a boys' school camp, when the assistant headmaster came to him, and with a grave face and a murmur of sympathy handed him an overseas copy of *The Times*. One glance at the page at which the paper had been opened was enough. There was the picture of a tall London building in flames, and beside it a news item entitled BIBLE MISSION EXPLOSION.

The first words of the report, 'An explosion in the three-

---

* There was one loss of life in the fire. A BBC Maltese language broadcaster, whose charred body was found in the ruins two days later. He was the visitor to whom the translation assistant had been talking when the explosion occurred and who was thought to have escaped without injury.

storeyed building of Scripture Gift Mission', hit him like a
blow. He was horrified. There was a measure of relief as he
read on and saw that Mighell Smith had been interviewed
and had come up with typically concise information for *The
Times* reporter.

'Mr Smith, the assistant Secretary of Scripture Gift
Mission, said there were about fifty-five of the staff, most of
them women, in the building at the time of the explosion, and
all of them were accounted for.' Thank God for that – no one
missing! 'He estimated that the Bibles and Scriptural works
destroyed were worth about £50,000.'

'The work of the Mission,' he added, 'was to distribute
evangelical literature to countries overseas, and it supported
all branches of the Christian Church. Works printed in about
300 languages were sent out to some 9,000 missionaries.'

That summarised it pretty well, Norman Brown thought.
There would have been no time to explain that the Mission's
speciality was the production of what might be termed
"guided tours" through the Scriptures; booklets and leaflets
of carefully selected verses on a variety of subjects, produced
by Bible students for those who were largely ignorant of its
contents. The newspaper reporter would have shut his
notebook and turned elsewhere if Mighell Smith had spoken
about the compilations on such subjects as Sin, Fear,
Judgment, The Deity of Christ, His Cross, Forgiveness,
Eternal Salvation. It would have been of no interest to him to
learn how these compilations had been translated and
produced in hundreds of languages, that some of them were
the only portions of the Word of God thousands of people
would ever possess, and that the primary work of the Mission
was to provide those portions in smaller or larger quantities
to the people who would distribute them, one by one, where
they were needed.

There is a time for everything, and the time to enlarge on
the work the Mission had been doing was obviously not when
an eager reporter was on his toes to get his news off as soon as

possible. In the circumstances it was surprising that so much had been included.

'Distributing evangelical literature in about 300 languages to some 9,000 missionaries, in all branches of the Christian Church.'

Yes, that was what the Mission had been doing – until yesterday. But now it had all gone up in flames. And Norman Brown realised that so much of it could not be reckoned in terms of cash. The records and the partly completed translations, the lists of names and addresses of people all over the world, the files and the accounts – how to put a price on them? What could the Mission do in the face of such loss?

When he had recovered from the momentary sense of being stunned, Norman Brown went to the phone and put through an overseas call to Ashley Baker's home.

Yes, it was true. The buildings were gutted and soaked. The water from eighteen hoses had done as much damage as the fire it had put out. No, there would be no purpose in his coming back. There was nothing he could do. Better stay on as padre to the end of the camp, as arranged. By that time they would have a better idea of how to proceed and get things re-started.

Yes, it was a severe blow, no doubt about that. Ashley Baker did not try to disguise his reaction. He had been badly shaken. *But* . . . 'But the Lord's people have been wonderfully good, and already there are signs that God is going to overrule it all for His glory.'

And on that note Norman Brown said goodbye, and replaced the receiver.

2

These Seventy Years

The fire of 23 April, 1956, has well been described as the
watershed in the history of Scripture Gift Mission. Like the
silhouette of a steep range of mountains, it sharply divided
the first seventy years of the Mission's existence from those
that followed, although the aim of the Mission remained the
same. That had not changed.

'I determined that in future, as far as I was able, with God's
help, I would devote my energies to the dissemination of the
Scriptures,' the founder had written away back in the reign of
Queen Victoria, and the story of how he reached that decision
and carried it out bears repeating.

William Walters, a printer in Birmingham, had become
aware that although there was quite a spate of evangelical
literature coming off his press, it was mainly for a limited
section of the Christian public. Very little was being produced
for those who did not come into that category. What was
being done for the millions who knew next to nothing of what
the Bible itself contained? And was it not more important
that people should read the Bible than what others wrote
about it?

That led on to the realisation that very few people wanted
to read the Bible anyway, and no wonder. Its appearance
often was so unattractive! As a printer and publisher he knew
the importance of pleasing the eye as a prelude to informing
the mind, yet here was the Word of God all too often being

produced with type so small and bindings so drab as to deter rather than attract readers.

Something must be done to rectify the situation, and William Walters set about doing it. Clear type and attractive bindings, important as they were, he felt were not enough, and as he thought and prayed about it, a seed of inspiration was sown in his mind. Clear type and pictures? Illustrations? These sometimes appeared in the huge old family Bibles that were to be found in most homes, and were only brought out to look at on Sundays or special occasions, but William Walters was thinking of books easy to handle, prepared for everyday use. Gospels, New Testaments, Bibles, with eastern pictures to attract the eye and bring things to life were what were needed. The illustrations must be of first-class quality, too.

So he employed talented artists for the job, even sending them to the Holy Land that they might reproduce scenes of the country itself. An eastern shepherd with his flock, women drawing water from a well, views of Palestine ... The pictures they painted were William Walters' most prized possessions, turning his office in Paternoster Row in the City of London (he had left Birmingham by this time) into a sort of miniature art gallery, to which a number of influential Christians found their way. They enthusiastically supported him in his aim of making the Bible available to all, even when it meant giving it away, and so, eventually, Scripture Gift Mission was born.

The official date of its inception was February, 1888. The first mention of it is of 'The Scripture Text Mission established for the free distribution of Scripture texts and Gospel books', but this somewhat cumbersome definition was soon summarised into the title under which it has always been known since. It was an organisation that produced copies of the Scriptures, and gave them away free of charge.

It attracted widespread attention in its early days, at one time encountering unexpected opposition on the part of those who objected to the Holy Scriptures being given away.

They ought only to be sold! Two or three newspapers were highly critical of the enterprise. On the other hand, it received royal patronage when, at the coronation of King Edward VII a copy of Mark's Gospel was presented to each of the one and a quarter million Londoners who were provided with a Coronation Dinner, while Queen Alexandra personally distributed New Testaments with their illustrations of the Holy Land to members of the court. One of the artists had become her art tutor, giving her an added interest in the Mission.

By this time it had launched out into the production of Scripture in other languages. The first of these was the Gospel of John in Arabic, published in response to the request of a wealthy ostrich farmer concerned for the Muslims of North Africa. It was followed by the Gospel of John in Spanish, the Gospel of Luke in French, the Gospel of Mark in Italian and the Gospel of John in Portuguese. As early as December, 1895, only seven years after its inception, the Mission was able to report that well over two million copies of the Gospels, half in English, half in the five other languages, had been printed. By 1910 it was issuing Gospels in 46 different languages, at the annual rate of a million and a quarter. Two years later the enterprising secretary, having heard that King George V, recently crowned, had promised his mother that he would read a chapter of the Bible every day, made discreet enquiries, and received the following answer from the King's secretary:

'I have had the honour of submitting your letter of the 15th inst. to the King, and I am directed to inform you, in reply, it is quite true that he promised Queen Alexandra, as long ago as 1881, that he would read a chapter of the Bible daily and that he has ever since adhered to this promise.'

The circulation, with royal permission, of this announcement, gave a nation-wide impetus to Bible reading and, incidentally, provided favourable publicity for SGM. When the 1914–18 Great War broke out and the Mission produced pocket Testaments and Gospels in English, French and Flemish for distribution among the Allied troops, Lord Roberts, Commander-in-Chief of the British Forces, wrote a foreword in his own hand, which was reproduced and printed in each one. It read:

> I ask you to put your trust in God. He will watch over you and strengthen you. You will find in this little Book guidance when you are in health, comfort when you are in sickness and strength when you are in adversity.

This was followed by a pocket edition for sailors, with words from the Admiral of the Fleet, Sir John Jellicoe, appearing in each one:

> Be strong and of good courage; be not afraid, neither be thou dismayed; for the Lord thy God is with thee whithersoever thou goest. Honour all men. Love the brotherhood. Fear God. Honour the King.

> Yours very truly,

> J. W. Jellicoe

Scripture Gift Mission with its incorporated society* distributed over 43,000,000 New Testaments, Gospels and booklets during the First World War. The readiness with which its productions were received, the eminent people who were prepared to add their names to them, and the financial support it received from wealthy donors during the early part of the twentieth century reflects the prevailing attitude towards the Bible at that time. It was respected, even by those who had no personal faith in its message, and the Mission which perhaps more than any other had disseminated it seemed set to increase more and more.

*The Naval and Military Bible Society was incorporated with SGM in 1910.

As things turned out, the reverse was the case. Popularity is a very uncertain vehicle on which to ride, and so is the patronage of princes. In the years that followed the First World War some hard lessons had to be learned. Finances were low, requests for much needed Scriptures had to be refused for lack of funds to produce them, and there was one occasion when the workers were asked to accept a cut in their salaries. The national trade depression and heavier taxation were the apparent reasons for the situation, but in later years the cause was seen to lie deeper. When the apostle Paul wrote to the Ephesians about being God's handiwork, and devoting ourselves to the good deeds for which God has designed us, he probably had individuals in mind. Yet the same principle seems to apply to organisations, too. The history of Scripture Gift Mission bears it out. It was to the dissemination of the Scriptures, and the Scriptures alone, that William Walters had dedicated himself, and as later events proved, any deviation of the Mission from that aim simply did not work. In the period following the First World War, efforts were made to improve finances by the sale of religious books – good in themselves, but not coming into the category of the dissemination of the Scriptures. The efforts proved useless and had to be abandoned. The acquisition of the lease of the property built by the late Lord Radstock as a chapel and Christian conference centre held promise of the SGM becoming a focal point for other societies, but the other societies were not interested in renting accommodation there, so that was a disappointment, too.

By the year 1933 finances were at a very low ebb, and humanly speaking there seemed little prospect of the situation being improved by the appointment of Ashley Baker to direct the work as Secretary. He had no personal connections in well-to-do or influential circles, having started in the Mission as an office boy – 'an intelligent little fellow in knickerbockers'. He had worked his way up to an administrative position, and with over a quarter of a century's experience knew every aspect of the Mission's activities, but as a fund raiser he was a non-starter.

'We don't raise funds – we bring them down' became a catchword in the Mission in later years, but it started when Ashley Baker laid down as a condition that if he were to become Secretary, there were to be no more appeals to the Christian public, or anyone else for that matter, for funds. The only appeals were to be made to God. In short, the Mission was to adopt what had come to be known as the faith principle, on the lines laid down by such men as George Müller and Hudson Taylor. Prayer was the means by which funds were to be brought down – not raised.

Not everyone approved of the transition. 'This new faith business will never work' prophesied one member of the Council, and when the first year had passed, and contributions were seen to have been even lower than the previous year, it appeared that he was right. But there was one important factor which could not be overlooked. *The year had ended without there being one outstanding debt.* And so the principles were outlined for the future of the Mission that there should henceforth be:

1. No appeals for money.
2. No advertisements for contributions.
3. No publications other than in the words of Holy Scripture.

There was no dramatic outpouring of wealth following the decision, no spectacular business dealings in favour of the Mission, and it was not until 1936 that an increase in income was reported, along with the circulation of eleven and a half million publications in 168 languages in 128 countries. But the financial tide had turned, and the faith principle was seen to be working.

With the outbreak of the Second World War endurance was called for, too, what with the blackouts and the bombings, disrupted communications and an inevitably reduced staff, although the Mission headquarters escaped with a minimum of damage. A few shattered windows and dislodged slates were as nothing when adjacent buildings were being reduced to rubble. And when it was all over there was the paper shortage to overcome. What proved even more difficult to overcome was the strong conviction held by some that texts from none other than the King James Version of the Bible should be used in SGM handbooks and booklets in the English language. More modern translations were viewed with suspicion, and not until 1952 could it be reported that some publications were now available in more modern translations.

But now, in 1956, policies were clearly defined and adhered to. The faith principle concerning money was taken as a matter of course, the only mention of it being at the fifteen-minute staff prayer meeting with which each working day commenced. Apart from a maximum of 10 per cent for titles and sub-titles, all the wording in SGM productions was in texts from the Scriptures. Free grants were made whenever possible, not for widespread distribution, but to those who would pass the literature on discriminately. The work was proceeding smoothly, the breadth of its outreach reflected in the mail that arrived day by day, in huge bundles, from countries all over the world. There were branches established in India, Ireland, South Africa, Australia, New Zealand and Canada, and a sister organisation in the USA. The rather heavily constructed, ornate building with its deep-set narrow windows on the corner of Eccleston Street and Eccleston Place was the hub of it all, the storehouse of translations, records, accounts, and file after file of correspondence, the very heart of the Mission.

And now it was a charred, sodden ruin. The only thing that seemed to have withstood the blast was the stand outside the building in which was a huge Bible, opened at a fresh page every day.

Rather significant, really. The *Daily Express* reporter had been quite struck by it. Indeed, he had ended his report with the words, 'But untouched by the fire, in its glass case on the street corner, stood a big Bible, a little red arrow pointing to the text for the day, "*Take, my brethren, the prophets, who have spoken in the name of the Lord, for an example of suffering affliction, and of patience.*"'

Viewed retrospectively, there was something symbolic about that Bible. There was something symbolic, too, about the very first financial expression of practical brotherly concern that the Mission received, only a few minutes after the disaster occurred. One of the workers, emerging dishevelled from the crumbling building, was stopped by a West Indian, who pressed some money into her hand with a distressed expression of sympathy.

It was only a silver coin, but its value was without price. He was a worker in a nearby garage, and had sped along wanting to do something to help. The spontaneity and warmth of that action was like a shaft of sunlight on a cloudy day, and proved to be the forerunner of many others. As Ashley Baker said on the phone to Norman Brown the following day, 'The Lord's people have been wonderfully good.'

That very morning a cheque had been received for £4,000 from an elderly Council member, and among the many gifts that came pouring in later were some from children which were specially touching.

'My Daddy has told me of the big fire in London last Monday,' wrote a six-year-old. 'I would like to send these five sixpences from my money box to buy some more Bibles.'

'Last Friday was my ninth birthday and I was given some money as a present. I thought it would be nice to send five shillings to you to help to pay for some more of the books that were burned in the fire,' wrote another.

Gifts soon started coming in from overseas, too. Ashley Baker had notified each of the branches of what had happened by the simple expedient of wiring and cabling the words 'Isaiah sixty-four, eleven' and little more. A reporter in Toronto, Canada, got hold of it, turned up his Bible and read the words,

'Our holy and beautiful house, where our fathers praised thee, has been burned by fire, and all our pleasant places have become ruins.'

The press man promptly wrote a front page article, gleaned mainly from the pictures he had seen on the television, and entitled it ISAIAH SAVES CABLE RATES. One way and another, the news was getting round. The unaccustomed and unsought publicity provided by press, television and radio speeded the news the world over, to the mission stations and to the groups of national Christians who had contacts with SGM. The warmth of their anxious reactions was heartening.

But the day after the fire it was accommodation that was seen to be the urgent need. The London City Mission on the opposite side of the road had already made part of their premises available for as long as they were needed. Collins, a firm with which SGM had been associated, promptly offered the temporary use of a suite of offices in Piccadilly. Thankfully the offers were accepted, but what was needed was a building in the vicinity big enough to house all the departments, which could be rented on a long-term basis. As it happened, enquiries for just such a place had already been set on foot, since the lease of the property SGM was occupying was running out, and might not be renewed. Ashley Baker had been applying to estate agents for months, with no result. But the very day after the fire he received a letter, posted a day or two before, informing him that within four or five months number 2 Buckingham Palace Gardens, a stone's throw away, was to be vacated.

The timing of the arrival of that letter was so significant that it seemed like a divine token for good. As Ashley Baker also said to Norman Brown in that brief overseas telephone conversation, 'There are already signs that God is going to overrule all to His glory.'

Meanwhile work was going on in the gutted building, with men in gum boots and mackintoshes heaving and shoving among the charred and sodden ruins for whatever could be salvaged. Mighell Smith was in his element. He had been a fireman in the Second World War, and knew how to set about things. The other men were less experienced, but they enjoyed it all the same. Ken Andrewartha was quite disappointed when he was called off and sent to the warehouse in Clapham, where a makeshift office had temporarily become the Translations Department. It made a change from sitting at a desk, poring over manuscripts, to be messing about in piles of wet rubbish and retrieving whatever might be of value. There was even the remote possibility that that 15th century Erasmus New Testament he'd had in the place of honour on his desk might turn up somewhere...

It was a job requiring muscle as steel filing cabinets, bent and twisted, were prised out of the rubble and hauled across the road into the hospitable premises of the London City Mission. Deposited there, their contents could be examined before they were carted away. Those contents could be invaluable. When Ronald Young had wrenched and pulled at the jammed drawers and eventually opened them, he learned to handle the charred papers he found inside with the delicacy of a surgeon's hand – and with a similar instrument, a knife. Gently he would insert the blade between two charred pieces of paper, and with his head on one side peer to see if there was anything still legible. He did not try to pull the sheet out. Experience soon taught him that it would crumble if he did. It was a minor triumph if he could decipher a name and address and scribble it on the pad beside him: Stanley Rowe... Malaysia, Ken Price... Hong Kong, Pastor Mendies... Colombo, Brother Singh... Bangalore, and so on. Every time a new list was compiled letters would go out to the individuals concerned explaining that there had been a fire, all correspondence destroyed, 'so please will you let us know what you wrote about, and we will do our best to fulfil your requirements.'

And so the lists of overseas contacts were slowly and painstakingly compiled all over again. Some were supplied from the other branches, some from memory, some by the people themselves, hearing of the fire, who wrote in. And some, alas, were lost sight of altogether.

The Translations Department was the one that suffered most. All those files of correspondence, with their meticulous search for the right words, the translations just started, those partially done, those almost completed, representing the painstaking work of days, weeks, months, sometimes years of dedicated men and women in faraway deserts and jungles, mountains and plains...! For those working in the Translations Department their own lost labour was little compared with that of some of their correspondents. To have to write and ask them to start all over again – if and when their names and addresses could be found or remembered, anyway. Not all came to mind as readily as that of G. K. Harris in South Thailand came to the mind of Ken Andrewartha. There were others on the files from whom nothing had been heard for weeks, even months, and it was hard to remember them all. Of the twenty-six manuscripts that were destroyed in the fire, only twelve were eventually replaced. Someone had translated *Word of Truth* into the colloquial Arabic of Khartoum... *Stories of Abraham* in Swahili – who had sent that? What was the name and address of the missionary who had provided *Stories of the Lord Jesus* in Hiholo?...

It was the same story in the other departments, in varying degrees, although, providentially, some escaped unscathed. The Accounts Department, for instance, had come off more lightly than others, with less destruction by fire and water, so that the insurance companies were provided with accurate figures within a short time. The list of people receiving

regular information in the shape of a prayer letter was found
to be intact, too. This was treasure trove indeed! Within days
those who prayed because they believed God heard and
answered could be acquainted with the situation, and their
petitions, ascending in the Name of Jesus, would result in all
sorts of things being straightened out.

Joe Carroll, lying in hospital, missed all this. His face and
head were very sore, and every now and then the scorched
skin would come off in strips, hair and all. If his thoughts
were directed to lost files of correspondence at all, they were
directed by Eric Cook to those of the Young Sowers
League.* Eric Cook was in the same ward, and the YSL was
his department. Scores of children from all over the country
had sent in their answers to the papers set, and would be
waiting for the results, to know whether they had passed and
would therefore qualify for a New Testament or a Bible. Eric
Cook could not help wondering if those papers had been
preserved, if the names and addresses of the youngsters had
been found...

Joe and Eric were strong and healthy, and in spite of their
injuries they recovered quickly, and went off to convalesce.
As with others, spiritually the fire was an enriching
experience for Joe. Two or three years later he realised that in
another way it had turned out to his advantage.

By that time SGM had risen phoenix-like from the flames,
and was preparing to move into brand new, purpose-built
premises. The legal wrangles were over, the Gas Board were
paying half the costs, the insurance companies were
providing their share, gifts had poured in, and to crown it all,
the Mission had been granted a ninety-nine-year lease on the
same site at a nominal rent.

The position of the site was of inestimable value to an
organisation that cultivated worldwide as well as nation-wide
connections. Within three minutes' walk of Victoria Rail and

---

* This name was later changed to Young Searchers League.

Coach stations, easy of access from the air termini, it stood on a corner in a main thoroughfare where it could not fail to catch the eye. It was near enough to the Houses of Parliament and Buckingham Palace for the tourist to fit in a visit while he was seeing the sights. Altogether at the very hub of communications! It was the envy of many an enterprising business man.

'Why should SGM go on sitting on a gold mine, right there in central London?' demanded one of them rather indignantly, in a conversation with Mighell Smith. 'Why, it's a prime site.'

'It's a prime site, and we have a prime work to do,' retorted Mighell Smith with spirit, his eyes flashing. 'Why should businesses that are only out to make money have the right to all the best sites?' God had provided SGM with that site, and they were in business, too – the worldwide distribution of the Word of God was their business. And the new buildings were nearing completion, light and airy, complete with showroom and capacious storerooms, and offices equipped with every modern labour-saving device that would make for efficient working. SGM was entering a new era.

It was at this point that Joe received a surprise. He had fully recovered from the effects of the fire, and had almost forgotten about it when suddenly he received a phone call announcing that he was to receive £200 compensation for his injuries.

Two hundred pounds! He'd never had so much money in his life. What should he do with it? It did not take him long to decide. He would use it in taking a trip back to India.

3

To India

Joseph Carroll, Joe for short, always admitted that he had had a good start in life. Not that he was born into a wealthy family – quite the reverse. Not all Indians with English blood in their veins were well-to-do. He was one of eight children, and when times were hard even had to wear his mother's shoes to school, not having a pair of his own. How the family managed on the salary his father drew from the Christian Literature Press in Bangalore was little short of miraculous, for although it was an honest wage, and had the distinction of being paid regularly without argument or 'fines', it did not go very far when it came to educating as well as feeding them all. No, the good start Joe had in life lay in the character of his parents. His father, a godly man if ever there was one, sowed seeds in the minds of his children that bore fruit in later years. Grace before meals, the regular reading and memorising of Scripture – were part of the daily programme, and as one of the missionaries in the Brethren Assembly he attended said, 'When Carroll rises to pray, you know that God is there.'

Joe himself made quite a good impression as a lad, cheerfully going round at Christmas time selling calendars and cards to earn a little pocket money, and when his father died suddenly, he promptly left school at the age of fifteen and got a job in an insurance office to help support the family. It was when the Second World War broke out, and he joined the Army that he started on a different path, down which he

hurtled recklessly as he travelled on a hospital ship between
Bombay, Egypt, and the Middle East. The varied experiences
of the nine or ten years that followed eventually found him,
practically and spiritually, like the Prodigal Son, in a far
country. He was in England, a long way from his native India,
and now he was even out of a job and with nowhere to live.
The farmer in Devon, for whom he had been working, told
him that times were so hard he'd have to be laid off. Also, he
would have to move out of the room he'd been occupying,
and find lodgings somewhere else.

It was at this point of utter destitution that the good start
he had had in life proved its value. Those Scripture verses he
had learned came to mind – not condemning, but comforting.
'The Lord is my shepherd – I shall not want', had recurred
frequently, even during that long period when he had only
gone to a place of worship once a year. (For some obscure
reason, he had always made a point of doing so every New
Year's Eve.) Now, at the end of his own resources, he turned
again to the God of his father.

He knew the way back. That foundation of memorised
verses could point the way unerringly. If he truly repented of
the waywardness of the years, if he confessed his sins and
shortcomings and pleaded for forgiveness in Jesus' Name, he
would obtain mercy. On his knees by his bed in the farmer's
cottage, not without tears of shame and regret, he did just
that. And in his consciousness of acute, immediate need, he
also prayed earnestly that God would find him a job. If God
did that for him, it would be the tangible evidence that his
prayers had been heard.

The next day he was told of a nearby saw mill where there
might be something he could do, so he went along and was
taken on straight away. After that he often quoted a verse he
had learned in his youth,

I was young and now I am old, yet I have never seen the
righteous forsaken, or their children begging bread.

'Or their children begging bread.' That was where he came in – the offspring of the righteous. A farm labourer took him in as a lodger, and all that winter his working hours were spent in felling trees and sawing logs. He was earning his living, not begging his bread, and Sundays found him in a place of worship again.

Three years later he was in London, this time working for a rubber company, and going along to the monthly prayer meetings at Scripture Gift Mission in Eccleston Street. It was there that the door opened for him into what he had been desiring – to work in a Christian organisation. He was asked if he would be prepared to act as caretaker in the premises – look after the boiler, clean the floors, help carry the parcels, anything...

The salary for the job was only half what he was getting with the rubber company, but he accepted without any hesitation. It was the bottom rung of a ladder that was to lead him into the sphere for which he was best fitted, and to bring fulfilment beyond anything he had known, although to those with whom he was acquainted at the time it looked like a step down, not up. Only a caretaker, when he was already doing well in that rubber company, and with good prospects! But by this time Joe's priorities had been readjusted. He knew the difference between outward prosperity and inner riches, and was quite prepared to forego the one in order to obtain the other. There was a satisfaction in working alongside others who were chiefly concerned to disseminate the Word of God that he had never known in the timber company or the rubber firm, either. Those prayer meetings – only ten to fifteen minutes twice a day, but what they meant to him! All the staff attended, from the Secretary to the newest young recruit, and they sat round in an informal circle, taking turns to pray briefly, so that everyone had a chance.

'Thank you, Lord, for the legacy of £5,000 that came in the post this morning,' someone in the Accounts Department would exclaim, while another time it would be, 'Lord, we're going to have this bill for thousands of pounds before the end of the month. Please send it to us.'

Sometimes there would be anxiety about a member of staff who was ill. Shortage of staff for one reason or other, was always a problem, 'Lord, we desperately need two men to help with the packing. We can't cope with all the orders, and some of them must go off today. Lord, please send us two men – today!'

Joe especially noticed that prayer. He was in the packing department himself by that time, and knew how pressed they were. He ought not to have been surprised, but he was, when later that day two men turned up offering to help with the packing...

By the time he received news of the £200 compensation money he was thoroughly integrated into SGM, and although he decided to spend the money on a trip home to India, he bought a two-way ticket. He wanted to return to the same job. And while he was there, amidst all the excitement and flurry of meeting old friends, family reunions, visiting familiar childhood scenes, the consciousness of his calling persisted. As a packer in the warehouse at Clapham, where he had gone after the fire, he had time and time again handled Gospels, booklets, leaflets in Hindi and Urdu, Telegu and Tamil, packed them up and seen them taken off in Post Office vans en route for India. Now he was in a position to find out first hand more about SGM in India, and one of the highlights of his two months' visit was to meet personally the two women who were at the heart of it.

Neither of them was Indian. Both were from Great Britain, and had been working as doctor and pharmacist in a Church Missionary Society hospital in Sindh when they received by post a sample packet of booklets, including *The Way Of Salvation* in English. This simple compilation of Scripture verses, plainly outlining the facts of the Deity, humanity, death and resurrection of Jesus Christ, and how anyone believing in Him would be saved, immediately impressed them. It got over the very message they were trying to convey to the patients who came to their clinic, and it was small enough to enclose in postal packets of medicines that were being sent out all over Sindh. So they wrote to SGM in London for permission to get it translated and produced in the Sindhi language. That led on to further translations of SGM productions, and in 1942 they received a cable from London asking if they would take over responsibility for the whole of SGM's work in India.

By the time Joe went to visit them, they were settled in a spacious Church Missionary Society compound in Bangalore, his own city. There, in a beautiful garden with trees and flowering shrubs he found them in their living quarters, complete with offices, store, packing room and a chapel. A living evidence of the power of the Word of God was one of their assistants. This young Punjabi had been on his way to bathe in a sacred lake under a new moon, hoping somehow to find God there, when he saw in their garden a large poster with the words GOD IS LOVE on it. Just three words, but they arrested him. He turned in to learn more of the God he was seeking, was led to Christ, and later baptised – on a day of the new moon, not secretly in a sacred lake, but openly, in full view of crowds streaming by.

Missions and missionaries not being very popular in India after the country gained its independence, they wisely changed the word 'mission' into 'ministry', thereby retaining the familiar initials without giving offence. 'Since we started the work in 1950 God has supplied all the money needed for its upkeep here in India,' they told Joe, adding that SGM in London still paid most of the printing bills. They had all the information about their work at their fingertips.

'We print and distribute well over a million portions a year, in fifty languages, using thirteen different alphabets,' Mrs Junkison told him.

Dr Western, having worked as a medical missionary for twenty-seven years, now spent most of her time at her desk, scrutinising translations and reading proofs. But that was not all she did at her desk. *The Way Of Salvation* which had first alerted her attention to the effectiveness of the exclusive use of Scripture in producing guidance on specific subjects, had been compiled by an invalid whose health prevented her from going to China as a missionary. Now there was an increasing demand for similar publications and Dr Western was applying her mind to compiling them. Her knowledge of India, its people and its customs had influenced her in putting together relevant texts on some thirty subjects such as Eating and Drinking, Marriage, Lawsuits, etc., and the collection had been called *Everyday Life*. It was to prove the basis of courses on the Christian life in many other countries than India, and was only the first of several such handbooks that she added to SGM's reservoir of spiritual teaching.

As for Mrs Junkison, her energy and enthusiasm for distributing the Word of God was infectious. 'I gladly gave up my work as a pharmacist to do it,' she told Joe. 'And when you had that fire in London, we here in India were able to help. We had good art pulls of all publications printed in India, and could supply what was needed for distribution of Indian languages in other countries.

'And so the work went on!'

The way the work continued in spite of all sorts of obstacles was a triumphant theme with her. She recollected the terrible days of partition in 1947, when India and Pakistan assumed dominion status, each with its own Governor-General, and the Union Jack was lowered in each country. She and Dr Western were in a hill station near the Himalayas at the time, and horrifying rumours started reaching them of what was happening in the Punjab. The Sikhs had risen, and were exterminating the Muslim minority! 'And we have friends on both sides!' Then they saw trails of smoke rising from scattered villages on the plains below. They knew only too well what it meant. The villagers were being massacred and their homes burnt. They saw little groups of people with frightened eyes hurrying down from the mountain sides with their cattle, and knew that in all likelihood death awaited them at the bottom. 'There was nothing we could do, but pray... We were cut off from the world, except by radio.'

Weeks later they were back in their compound in the Punjab, but how different everything was. True, there was a pile of clean clothes waiting for them – but they never saw the washerman again. He had been killed. A newly made dress had been delivered in their absence – but their friend the tailor had been killed, too.

'Instead of the scent of the sweet clover fields and mustard fields, there was the smell of blood-soaked earth. And again we were cut off. Trains were not running, and there was no post.

'Then came the day when God said plainly "Leave your home and go south. Ask for Army transport." It was a terrible wrench. Quite suddenly the iron ring round us opened, and within a week we were being driven in our car by a young British officer to Delhi, and behind us in a three-ton lorry were our possessions, everything necessary for the carrying on of SGM's all-India work from Bangalore, 2,000 miles away.'

And when, at the close of the financial year they sat down to assess what had been done, they found that in spite of everything they had had printed in India 380,000 portions in eighteen languages, including two new ones, and that distribution had kept pace with production. 'The drop in distribution in the north had been balanced by an increase in other parts, especially the south.' God had seen to it.

And so – the work went on!

In the midst of those terrible months there was one message that had come to them again and again. 'You may ask me for anything in my name, and I will do it.' They had been fearful that the production and distribution of the Bibles, Gospels, and booklets would be held up by the chaotic conditions, but on the basis of that divine message they had prayed and their prayers had been heard. (The same thing had happened in London, for exactly one year after the fire Ashley Baker had been able to report that a greater number of Scriptures had been sent out than ever before.)

Mrs Junkison was a born story teller, and had vivid word pictures of the effect of the Word of God on lives in all sorts of remote and unlikely places which held Joe spellbound. There was the case of the quiet, hard-working Muslim who was employed by a Hindu in one of the small native states, who saw a man selling books in the market one day, and bought one for half an anna. It was the Gospel of John in his own language. Fifteen years later, in the same market place, a colporteur selling Bibles and SGM handbooks, was surprised to be approached by a man, obviously a Muslim, who picked up one of the books and said to him, 'I have been reading a book like this, and living by it for fifteen years, and I believe in Jesus Christ.' He was prepared to give evidence of his faith by being baptised, but in spite of the fact that he was now known as a Christian, the trader he worked for valued him so highly that he continued to employ him.

Then there was the case of a low caste Hindu who bought a copy of *Saviour Of The World* in a market because it looked like good value for money. He couldn't read very well, so he struggled through it once without grasping its meaning, but he thought to himself, 'I have paid for this, so I must read it again and get the meaning.' So he read it again and again, and gradually its message sank into his heart. 'If this Jesus of the Book is true,' he told his family, 'we must leave our idols.' He read it aloud to them, and to cut the story short, when a travelling evangelist arrived in that village some time later, he found four families all asking for baptism. 'This book got hold of my heart,' the man said.

'But that book was in large print,' Mrs Junkison observed. 'The man was practically illiterate, and if it had been in smaller print he might never even have read it. We always have to bear in mind the fact that the vast majority of people in India are, at best, semi-literate. They would be put off from reading anything with small print. What's more, they read so slowly, it would hamper their understanding if there was too much. That's one reason why SGM productions are so suitable. The selected texts are easy to understand, and all relevant to the subject.'

Joe nodded, listening eagerly. He had been in England so long now that he had almost forgotten this matter of widespread illiteracy in the land of his birth, and how it affected the manner in which literature was produced. There were other aspects of production, too, that she could bring to his attention. *The Way Of Salvation* was a booklet with which he was very familiar. He'd seen it in piles on the shelves in the warehouse in Clapham in many different languages, produced with variations of appearance to suit the different cultures. Now he found himself looking at it in the language of Tibet, and he noticed that the shape of the booklet was different from others. It was narrow and oblong, not squarish as were most. That was the shape in which the sacred writings of the Lamas were produced, he was told, and would therefore command attention as being a sacred book. The colour was chosen with that in mind too. Dark red.

'Our flow of books, and of the newspaper, into Tibet, has been stopped by events there, with the Chinese Communists gaining control...'

Tibet?

But had not Tibet always been a closed country? Hadn't it always been closed to Christian missionaries? Hadn't the famous Sadhu Sundar . Singh, the converted Sikh, been thrown into a pit and left for dead when he entered with the Gospel, and was only delivered by a miracle? And hadn't he eventually lost his life, trying to take the message of the living Saviour into the land?

Yes, that was true. "The Roof of the World", as Tibet was sometimes called, had been under the control of the Dalai Lama, priest-king of the country, for centuries, and missionaries were forbidden to enter. But that had not stopped the Word of God from getting in. Mrs Junkison could tell of ways in which the little red book *The Way Of Salvation* had been taken in by traders, visitors, by Tibetans coming down into India and returning with copies given to them there. There had even been a newspaper printed in Kalimpong in the Tibetan language and distributed in Lhasa itself, and as the printer was a Christian he had seen to it there was always a Christian message inserted in his newspaper. That door was closed now. The newspaper could not get in, nor the booklets either.

'But the work has gone on! Thousands of refugees are coming over the Tibetan border into India now, and we have sent books to various districts for the use of local Christians who are eager to have a share in the distribution. Even the Dalai Lama himself, who escaped from Lhasa and is now in North India, has received some books. Opportunities come, but they do not last for ever, and we must take full advantage of them while we can – then be on the lookout for new ones!'

Mrs Junkison's contacts ranged far and wide, and just now she was full of the openings in Assam.

'During the past two years we've issued four Scripture publications for the Vaiphei tribe, including *Love and Obedience*, a study of the Ten Commandments taken from both Old and New Testaments. These people live in thatched houses built on stilts on hilltops surrounded by bamboo jungle or dense forest. Some Christians in the tribe call themselves the Vaiphei Gospel Band, and by preaching, using Gospel records and SGM literature they take the Good News to the villages.

'The Daphla tribe, too. We've recently published *The Good Shepherd* in their language – our first booklet for them.' She had the snapshot of one of the tribesmen reading it, squatting on his haunches, bamboo quiver of arrows on his back, along with a knapsack fastened to his coil of hair by a skewer.

'Lost sheep, he and his fellow-tribesmen!' she said looking at it thoughtfully. 'May they find the Lord Jesus is truly the Good Shepherd!'

From time to time news reached her of someone actually coming to a personal knowledge of Christ as Saviour through reading an SGM booklet, and when that happened her spirits soared. She had recently heard of such a case that had happened years before in Pakistan, and related it with enthusiasm now.

'He was a railway clerk, and a Muslim. But he was one who really longed to know God, and in his way had been seeking Him for seven years. At last he went to the headquarters of the Ahmadiyas at Rabbwah, in Pakistan. As you know, it's about the most anti-Christian sect of Muslims there is. Well, while he was there someone put into his hands a copy of *The Coming King*. Dr Western compiled it,' she added with pride. She was always quick to give credit to her fellow-worker. 'Well, this booklet was in Urdu, which he understood, and he read it through. Somehow he realised this was just what he had been seeking. He went straight to the MIK Christian Publishing House to find out more. After a time he was baptised. This happened in 1952, and I've since heard that he is going on well.'

Joe's visit to India had been planned as far as he was concerned to see his family and satisfy his natural longing for his own country and his own people. He did not realise at the time that another purpose was being fulfilled. Among his vast store of memorised Scripture verses was one which instructed him to 'trust in the Lord with all thine heart and lean not to thine own understanding. In all thy ways acknowledge Him, and He shall direct thy paths.' His paths were being directed, and his use of his £200 compensation money proved later to be part of a Divine plan. He returned to England with a deepened sense of involvement in the whole work of the Mission into which he realised he had been led – an involvement that reached far beyond his job of packing parcels in the warehouse at Clapham.

Meanwhile, the Mission itself was entering a new era, with the retirement of Ashley Baker.

The fifty years which he had served in it had witnessed some of the most significant events in world history. The Second World War had ushered in the uneasy new age of nuclear power, with all its potential for development or destruction. Colonialism was dying, with country after country obtaining independence and raising its own flag. One small area at the eastern end of the Mediterranean had re-emerged with the ancient name of Israel. Commercial airlines were bringing the ends of the earth within reach of each other, while the rise of nationalism was splitting them apart. It was a new age and new methods were called for.

The year 1960 saw the beginning of them. It started with a drastic cut back. The Council decided to close the Business Department.

The Business Department, as its name suggests, was the department involved in selling Scriptures, Bibles, New Testaments, Gospels, calendars and greeting cards. Sold at a profit no one raised any objection to it. Nothing but good could come from distributing such literature, and since many people were eager to pay for these various publications, it seemed rank foolishness to cut off such a source of income. All the profits went towards the free literature the Mission existed to distribute anyhow. And now it was to be closed down! It seemed a very unreasonable thing to do, just as the new premises, with its strategically placed showroom, complete with excellent display windows, were being opened.

The announcement came as quite a shock, and met with a reaction of dismay and disappointment from many supporters who used the Mission's high quality publications for suitable presents, especially at Christmas.

But the Council had in mind the Mission's aim – 'The evangelisation *of the world* by the Word of God'. When it was suggested a year or so after the fire, that the personnel and

facilities of the Business Department could perhaps be used
to better advantage in assisting the missionary side of the
work, the Council considered the matter at length.

As other organisations in Great Britain were now
producing and distributing similar publications SGM could
retire from that field, and concentrate its attention where
there was a far greater need. With more than half the
population of the world still in ignorance of God and His
offer of everlasting salvation, there could be little doubt as to
where the greater need lay.

The Mission must take a new look at the world, and the
areas where there was a dearth of the Word of God. National
and international conditions were changing rapidly and
unpredictably. Doors that stood wide open one day could
close the next, and if opportunities were not grasped when
they occurred, they might disappear for ever.

At the Council meeting held on Friday, 19 August, 1960, it
was agreed, as a matter of future policy, 'To concentrate on
missionary distribution...'

4

To the Far East

On the face of it, the job of an Area Secretary at SGM was
rather a mundane affair. It meant arriving at HQ by 9 a.m. in
time for prayer, then going off to one's office, with its steel
filing cabinets and wire trays, its maps and its charts, and
sitting at a desk for the rest of the day, answering telephone
calls and meeting visitors, reading reports and dictating
letters. The prime responsibility was to establish and
maintain contact with organisations and individuals using
SGM material in the particular part of the world which
comprised one's area, and that is what Ronald Young had
been doing up to the time of the fire. He was Area Secretary
for Europe and the Middle East, having arrived at that
position by an apparently unimportant incident which might
never have occurred at all.

It happened in 1954. He wanted the address of someone in
Switzerland, and finding himself in the vicinity of Victoria
decided to go and see if Mighell Smith, whom he knew
slightly, could supply it.

Mighell Smith, genial and helpful as ever, invited him into
his office, supplied the address, then enquired in a friendly
way how the Alliance Club was getting on. This was a
recently opened hostel for students, mainly from overseas, he
knew Ronald Young was its warden. The Club was going
well, he was told, then in the course of conversation he
learned that Young had only agreed to act as warden until it

was on its feet, and had now left. He and his wife had moved out just at the end of last week actually, Ronald added casually.

So what were they going to do now?

They were looking to the Lord to show them the next step, he said, rather reluctant to talk about his own affairs. That was not what he had come for.

Whatever Mighell Smith felt at that unexpected revelation he kept to himself, merely asking conversationally, 'Have you ever met Mr Ashley Baker? No? Come along and let me introduce you.'

In the brief chat that ensued, a few details of their visitor's life came out. He'd been in the Middle East during the war – Egypt and Palestine. Yes, he'd met some of the missionaries working there. After leaving the forces he'd taught in a school in Jerusalem, and during that time he'd used some of the publications SGM produced in Arabic. He had to admit that that was all he knew about SGM. They were ready to supply, free of charge, very well-produced portions of Scripture in other languages, as well as in English, and as a young missionary on a limited budget he had been grateful to take advantage of their offer. He'd done what he could while he could, but his opportunities had soon come to an end. Much of the last three months of his time in Jerusalem had been spent in a cellar under mortar fire between Jews and Arabs just before the end of the mandate in 1948. By that time things had become so hot for the British that he and his colleagues were ordered out – His Majesty's Government could take no responsibility for them if they remained. After that he had gone to university, then to the Alliance Club for a limited period.

If Ashley Baker and Mighell Smith had exchanged glances at this point in the conversation, Ronald Young hadn't noticed it, but a short time later he learned that SGM had been looking and praying for an Area Secretary for the Middle East, and that as far as they were concerned, they

believed Ronald Young was the man for the job. Had he any
reason to believe this was not the guidance that he had been
praying for?

The outcome was that he had started work there on the
following Monday, and had been at it until the fire, with
Europe and the Middle East as his responsibility. The day
after the fire he was invited to extend his activities to include
the Far East. The Translations Department had suffered
most from the explosion, and would need additional help to
get it back in working order. The Far East Area Secretary was
exceptionally gifted in checking manuscripts, so he was to
join the translation team, leaving his Area Secretaryship
vacant. The idea was for Ronald to take it on as well as his
own.

So, of course, he took it on. It involved a lot more work,
with increasing demands on his mind and his memory and, as
he was to find, on his emotions too, although that did not
come until later. The early years inevitably had their periods
of strain as well as of satisfaction, and there were times when
he found himself stretched to the limit of his capacity, when
he faced a pile of correspondence with a secretary who was off
sick, or with no secretary at all. Staff shortages were a
perennial problem. But it was with the introduction of the
new era that fresh demands were made on his emotions. They
came about when it was decided that the Area Secretaries
ought to go and see for themselves where and how SGM
literature was being used. His field being the Far East, it was
there that he should go.

He did not deny that the prospect of doing so was wholly
inviting, and he set about planning his itinerary.

His contacts at that time were almost entirely with
missionaries. The Christian and Missionary Alliance in
Bangkok, Overseas Missionary Fellowship in Malaysia and
Singapore, Brethren missionaries in Hong Kong, and so on.
He wrote ahead, making arrangements, and eventually
boarded a Comet one day in March, 1960, bound for

Bangkok. A few hours later the plane was taxiing to a standstill on the tarmac of the airport, and he saw for the first time how East and West were meeting and merging, with little thatched bamboo houses on stilts and air conditioned modern buildings cheek by jowl, and open air markets sprawling near highways along which cars, lorries, and buses rumbled noisily, exuding their fumes. He had arrived in Asia, the continent in which lived two thirds of the world's population – Asia, with its picturesque diversity and its ancient religions, its teeming plains and its mountain fastnesses, its patience and its pain.

He did not see much of the pain at first. His time was taken up with discussions about production, translation, distribution, visits to missionaries he had been corresponding with, and what was to prove of strategic importance in the future, introductions to national Christians.

Perhaps a vague prophetic instinct enabled him to foresee how complex the situation was to become for expatriate workers in countries where formerly there had been no objection to them settling. Perhaps it was the wise realisation that the most effective way of distributing the Word of God was through those in whose language it was being produced, those born and bred in the land. Perhaps it was merely the spontaneous reaction of an out-going nature that caused him to seize the opportunity to become acquainted with pastors and evangelists in Thailand, Malaysia, Hong Kong. Whatever may have been the reason, the fact is that it was on this first trip to the Far East that he started to build up the long list of names and addresses which later was to form the basis of his wide circle of friends and acquaintances there, and ensure open doors for SGM literature into areas which were later closed to missionaries.

However, at that time missionaries were having unusual opportunities in the lands that had recently gained independence from British, Dutch, and French colonialism. Heartening reports were reaching Bangkok of a spiritual

awakening in Laos, Cambodia and Vietnam. In Phnom
Penh, capital of Cambodia, the response to the Gospel which
had previously been very slow was now accelerating faster
than the missionaries on the spot could cope with. In Saigon
it was the same. With its concentration of military forces and
the threat of the Communist invasion from the north, the fear
and tension underlying the outward gaiety of the city had
created an atmosphere in which many were facing the issues
of life – and death. The demand for Christian literature
exceeded the available supply, and Ronald time and time
again made grants that challenged his faith and his sometimes
rather desperate prayer that the money would come in to
meet the bills when they fell due.

Travelling down the Malay peninsula he visited some of
the missionaries who had been withdrawn from China after
the Communist take-over, and had settled in the new villages
that had been formed for Chinese plantation workers in the
jungles of Malaysia. Here the going was harder, but as he
walked round a tin-roofed open market where the missionary
had set up a screen and projector and was openly proclaiming
the Gospel, he smiled to himself with satisfaction as he saw
how many, lurking on the outskirts of the crowd, were
slipping SGM booklets into their pockets when they had the
opportunity.

It was in Saigon that the strain on his emotions began, for
here he was taken to a huge military hospital, where
helicopters were landing in the grounds, bringing in the
wounded. He had been taken especially to attend the regular
Gospel service that was held in the cinema, to which hundreds
of the wounded soldiers came, many in wheel chairs, some
even on stretchers. He looked at those young men, many of
them maimed for life, saw them listening eagerly to the only
message of hope that could be held out to them, and was told,
'We use SGM publications for counselling the enquirers after
the meeting.'

Back in London those passages of Scripture had been

carefully selected, translation painstakingly checked, to be produced in Saigon in the Vietnamese language. Here he was seeing where they got to, saw some of the hands outstretched to receive them, bandaged hands of teenaged boys, with bodies broken. 'That's the only bit of the Word of God they've got.' It moved him nearly to tears. But there was one incident which he never forgot, and could describe vividly a quarter of a century later.

His escort was taking him round the wards after the meeting – purpose-built wards, but stark and bare, with their tin roofs and concrete walls. They came to a bed on which a Vietnamese officer was lying, seriously wounded, and on the pillow at his head were two objects – a very honourable medal, and a copy of *Tin Lanh* (Good News). He had been in an armoured personnel carrier when it hit a land mine, exploded, and he was thrown into the ditch. When he recovered from the shock he peered out, and saw that an enemy machine gun was being fired down the road on which one of his friends was lying, unconscious. He crawled out of the ditch towards his friend, to drag him out of the line of fire, and in doing so was seriously wounded himself. His first contact with the Gospel message was in the military hospital, as he lay helpless on his bed. The words he heard were these, 'Greater love has no one than this, that one lay down his life for his friends.'

He looked up at Ronald and said, 'I nearly did that – but Jesus actually did it for me.'

One of the worst disasters that ever hit Hong Kong was the great fire in the squatters' camp at the Christmas period of 1959. Thousands upon thousands of refugees from mainland China had sped over the border, flooding into the colony and then finding there was nowhere for them to live except on the bare hillsides, they had built there for themselves such shelters as they could contrive. The squatters' camps were made up of a jumble of old tents, planks of wood, odd mats, old carpets, sacking, strips of lino, anything that could be held together by string and twine to provide a modicum of shelter from wind and rain. By the winter of 1959 the biggest of these camps was spread along a hillside overlooking the harbour, like a sore eye on the face of Hong Kong – and as painful. At night tiny specks of light could be seen here and there – little open fires on which evening meals were being cooked. And it was presumably one of these that got out of control, so that in a matter of minutes flames were darting from one flimsy home to another, and Hong Kong had the horrifying view of what at a distance looked like a forest fire.

But Hong Kong knew that that particular forest fire was full of human beings, defenceless, trapped in the flames.

Ronald arrived in Hong Kong shortly after this tragedy, and saw some of the aftermath. The streets were fairly normal during the day, bustling, crowded with people hurrying here and there, intent on their business, but when night came and they disappeared into their homes, the streets took on another aspect. Little groups of people appeared rather stealthily, carrying baskets and bundles, to settle in shop fronts, on the steps of public buildings, up the stone stairways of blocks of flats. He saw some arriving with huge cardboard boxes, carefully folded, and open them up on deserted pavements, to sleep until morning broke, then fold them up and carry them away. Where? He did not know. The refugees, he was told, were allowed to sleep in the shelter of the city at night, but had to move off during the day.

It was witnessing that sort of thing that strained his emotions – that, and meeting people like Mrs Donnithorne.

Mrs Donnithorne and her husband, the Archdeacon, had been missionaries in China for about thirty years until the general evacuation of missionaries from that land, and now they were established in Hong Kong, where the indefatigable

Mrs Donnithorne was promptly immersed in a variety of activities, mainly among the refugees. The refugee children especially claimed her attention. Something must be done about their education, but where could they be housed in order to be educated? The only available spaces in the over-crowded colony seemed to be on the roof tops, so to the roof tops she went – the flat roofs of the blocks of flats that were rapidly being erected. With makeshift desks, the minimum of equipment and hastily recruited teachers, she got the schools started, and eagerly took Ronald to see one of them. He noticed that she was quite bent, and rather frail.

'We want them to learn to read, and we want them to read the Word of God,' she explained as they started to mount the first flight of stone stairs. 'And we want them to have it for themselves. Those Bible stories you produce, they are just right for them.

'But it's not only the children – it's their parents,' she continued as they mounted the second flight of stairs. 'That booklet of yours called *Daily Strength*. If the children can take copies of that back to their parents, what it will mean to them!' They had reached the third floor by now, and Mrs Donnithorne stopped.

'I want to look at that text. I always stop here and look at it,' she said. Ronald looked round for a text on the bare concrete wall, but saw none. 'Which text?'

'As thy days, so shall thy strength be,' said Mrs Donnithorne rather breathlessly, but with a bright smile. 'I always stop here and look at it.' After a few moments' pause she started climbing again, and on the fifth floor announced, 'I want to stop and think about that text...' And so she got to the top, and he saw the orderly crowd of dark-haired, bright-eyed Chinese children gathered around the young teacher, listened to them singing choruses for his benefit, looked with his heart full at the little bundle of booklets he had brought with him being handed round and grasped excitedly – those well-chosen compilations of Scripture verses in Chinese.

She took him to the Walled City, too. It was not at all what he had expected, with a name like that. Instead of seeing a sort of impregnable fortress-like pile of buildings in the middle of a plain, he was taken to an ordinary looking row of typically eastern-type open-fronted shops in a street just like many other streets he had seen in Hong Kong. 'Here we are,' said Mrs Donnithorne, and disappeared into a narrow, dark alley between two shops. Down, down he went after her, down narrow, greasy steps into the dim interior of the medley of shacks and buildings, cobbled lanes and open drains that until recently the authorities in Hong Kong had left strictly alone, allowing it to be a law unto itself, taking no responsibility for what happened within its precincts. Here the pimps and the prostitutes, the drug smugglers and the thieves could do what they chose, the dens for opium smoking and gambling could operate unlicensed, secret societies and gangs could carry on their vendettas without government interference. The pool of humanity hidden behind the surrounding façade of shop fronts had been left to make its own arrangements for living and for dying, and as far as Mrs Donnithorne knew she was the first Western woman to enter it.

She had gone to see how best the light of the knowledge of God could be introduced and her advent had met with a guarded response. 'Do-gooders' were rare in the Walled City, and were viewed with suspicion or contempt, so there were times when refuse tipped out of windows coincided with the passing by directly underneath of 'the foreign devil'.

What did she do when that happened, Ronald wanted to know.

'As a Christian, what is there to do?' was Mrs Donnithorne's cheerful reply. 'I just smile up at them!' She had obviously won her way through, for she had established a school for children, a soup kitchen for the hungry, and now a Chinese pastor came once or twice a week to preach in a room rented for the purpose at the crossing of two main alleys.

SGM posters adorned the walls, and SGM leaflets were
available at the meetings, in the soup kitchen, and in the little
schoolroom. 'People soon forget what they hear. What they
need is something in their own possession that they can read
over and over again,' Ronald was told. 'This is where your
leaflets are invaluable. They contain the Word of God in
small doses, easily digested, exactly suited to their condition.'
For the preaching hall to be without them was like opening a
dispensary that was devoid of medicines.

It was the same out in the typhoon shelter, where the
Oriental Boat Mission's vessel was harboured among the
boats crammed with refugees from China. The sick people
who came to the Mission's clinic, the illiterate who attended
the Mission's classes, went back to their crowded quarters
carefully holding colourful leaflets in their hands, to pore
over them at their own pace, absorb the words, get the
meaning, make their response... 'Lives are being changed.
One sees the difference. It is not in vain.'

What Ronald saw and heard on that first journey into Asia
made worth while all the hours spent in committee rooms or
with publishers, working over the mechanics of literature
production. The decision to send Area Secretaries on
personal visits to their respective fields was yielding a two-
way result. Not only were contacts being made that were
extending the use of SGM material where it was most needed,
but the workers in London headquarters were receiving fresh
insights at first hand which served to strengthen their own
conviction that it was God's work they were doing.

It was that conviction that kept some of them in SGM for a
lifetime.

5

And Eastern Europe

It is usually only in retrospect that the evidence of a
predestined course in life becomes clear, and it is unlikely that
Ken Andrewartha had any idea, when he listened enthralled
to the missionary from the Ukraine, that he was receiving a
directive for his life work. He was only a schoolboy at the
time, cheerfully attending a meeting in his church. His plans
for the distant future were vague and unformed, healthy
anticipation of the next football match, and apprehensions
about the end of term exams bounding the horizon of his
mind. But he came away from that meeting with a vision he
never forgot. The speaker, Stewart Hine, the man who
translated the hymn 'How Great Thou Art' from Russian into
English, had opened up a new vista before him – the
possibility of serving God among the people of eastern
Europe.

The next turn in the course of his life came when he
enrolled for his two years of National Service, and was
drafted to Austria, where the Allies were to maintain a
presence for ten years after the end of the Second World War.
There, in a village near the Hungarian border, his only
English companion was another young soldier. The rest were
the Austrian villagers, the Russian soldiers billeted a short
distance away, and the strings of refugees, mainly of German
origin, who came almost daily across the border into Austria.
The eighteen months he spent there made him aware of the

people of a vast area that before had only been to him a blob on a map: Hungary, Romania, Russia, Czechoslovakia, and especially Yugoslavia with its inhabitants from such varied places as Macedonia and Montenegro, Serbia and Croatia. He was on good terms with all of them, picked up phrases in their languages, enjoyed their folk songs, and started learning German in earnest.

He found he had a flair for languages, so when his term of National Service was completed and it was time to go to university, he chose languages as his subject, concentrating on German and Russian. He did not know what for, but greatly influenced by the Christian Union at Cambridge, hoped it would be in some form of Christian work.

While still a student he went back to Austria for a year – not to a border village, but as a teacher of English in the picturesque city of Vienna, with its rich history of culture – and intrigue. He formed some lifelong friendships with Austrian fellow-believers there, and before returning to England he paid his first visit to a Communist country. He went into Yugoslavia for a fortnight and fell in love with it. Then he returned to England, and having obtained his post-graduate certificate in education was looking for a job when he heard that SGM was looking for a translations checker. It did not take them long to realise they had found each other.

So that is how he entered his life work. By the time of the fire, two years later, he was firmly established in the Translations Department, having his mind and vision extended under the guidance of Archie Long to regions far beyond the limits of his own experience. The year after joining the staff of SGM he was sent to a Wycliffe Bible Translators linguistics course at Chigwell in Essex. There, in the rugged living conditions of that early camp, he met men and women who shared their experiences of life in remote areas of Africa, Asia, South America, among primitive tribes, some of whose tongues had to be reduced to writing before any Bible translation could be attempted. To provide them with the very first portions of Scripture in their own language would be an inestimable privilege, he thought.

One story he heard from an elderly missionary in the Qua Iboe Mission especially affected him. It was of a man of the Lobi tribe in Africa, in whose heart was a desire to know the Unseen God who he vaguely felt existed somewhere, he did not know where. His handmade idols did not satisfy him. One night he had a strange experience. He was sleeping on the roof of his low hut when he was awakened to find himself rolling off unhurt to the ground. This happened three times, and the thought came to him that God was attracting his attention. Awed but expectant, he waited. Then came to him the words, 'Throw away your idols and I will send someone to tell you about Me.' So he threw them away and waited.

'I was the first messenger of Christ to reach that tribe,' the elderly missionary told Ken. 'And, not surprisingly, that man was the first to believe.'

Then he added rather solemnly, 'But do you know what he said to me? He told me that ten years had passed since he had that experience. Ten years of waiting. And the question he asked me was, "Why have you been so long in coming?"' Those words rang again and again in Ken's mind.

Why have you been so long in coming? Their challenge served many times as an impetus to offset the routine of sitting at a desk in an office near Victoria station, day after day, checking manuscripts. And that is what his work mainly consisted of for the first years he was in SGM.

Then it suddenly expanded. With his knowledge of some of the languages of eastern Europe, and personal acquaintances he had already formed there, it was decided he was the man to become the Area Secretary for that whole region. Some of his work in the Translation Department could be shared with others.

In some ways the new job kept him in the office as much as the old one, for it largely involved correspondence, telephone calls, and receiving the occasional visitor from eastern

Europe. But from time to time he arranged to go there himself, to meet personally some of the Christian leaders he had been corresponding with, and find out at first hand how best SGM could help them.

Even those personal visits, inspiring as it was to him to meet some whose Christian witness made them marked men, entailed very little risk or danger to himself. The chief purpose of them was to discuss such prosaic matters as format, size of type, and the most suitable selections of SGM publications for translation into the varied language groups of eastern Europe. Then came the more sensitive matter of consignments sent from London – to whom should they be addressed? Would their arrival focus too much attention on the recipient?

'Don't send many to me – the authorities will take note, and I don't want to ask for trouble. Here are a few other names and addresses – please distribute the consignments among them.' There were lists of names and addresses of those to whom a Bible or New Testament could be sent once every six months. 'By post. Just two a year – not more, for fear of arousing suspicion.' The recipients would quietly pass them on where they were most needed. 'Better send them by registered post. All too many that have been sent by ordinary mail have never reached their destinations. Stolen en route...'

There were other openings, too. The very first journey Ken made was only of four days' duration, into Yugoslavia, but it resulted in the publishing of some of SGM's Scripture selections in a monthly magazine published in Zagreb, and an arrangement with the Trans World Radio broadcasts from Monte Carlo to provide the Scriptures requested by listeners in the Serbo-Croatian area of the country.

'At present these are being sent from the modest stock available here, but it cannot last for long,' wrote Ken from Zagreb. 'I was asked if such requests could be sent on to SGM in London, and I replied in the affirmative without hesitation. These requests will therefore in due course start to reach us. They will be, I think, chiefly for New Testaments and Bibles.'

His reports were fully and carefully produced, but there were some things which never got into them at all.

Memory is not unlike a camera held in the hand of a skilled photographer who sees a picture in an unlikely place and snaps it secretly, to preserve for ever a fleeting incident. In the mental album of Ken's memory two or three of those fleeting and apparently unimportant incidents have been extracted and, so to speak, framed with words as he has related them from time to time.

The first was when he was sitting on a sun-clad hillside in Yugoslavia. Inland from the Dalmation coastline with its gleaming ports and fishing villages lies the region of Bosnia, and he was relaxing on the grass overlooking one of the towns there, his thoughts wandering idly. Then up from his subconscious mind came something he had read in an old book about that region. It was about the children. 'The children of Bosnia are exceptionally friendly.'

Exceptionally friendly children...

But that was years ago, he thought, before the ravages of war and civil war had blasted normal living and neighbourly relationships. 'I guess they're different now, after all they've gone through – the fear and the killing and the inhumanity they've seen. Must be suspicious of everyone...'

A pity, he reflected and wondered about the former children of Bosnia. He'd like to have met them. Unaware that anyone had approached him, he started when suddenly he heard a little voice behind him saying, 'Dobar dan...'

Turning his head in surprise he caught his breath at what he saw. Clad in white blouses and blue skirts and shorts stood a fair-haired girl and boy of about nine years old, with bunches of flowers in their hands, smiling shyly at him, unafraid. They were waiting, with all the innocent expectancy of childhood, for his response to their greeting.

'Dobar dan... good day!' He answered quickly, grinning cheerfully at them. He tried to make conversation, but his Yugoslavian vocabulary was strictly limited, and he could not get very far. However, he had some leaflets with him, attractively produced Bible stories in their own language, so he handed them one each, which they accepted, wide-eyed and happy. Then they moved off again, and he watched them wandering off down the hillside, a strangely nostalgic feeling possessing him. It was as though a curtain had been raised to reveal the children in the cities and the plains, the mountains and the steppes of eastern Europe. Smiling children, with all the innocent expectancy of childhood, waiting...

It moved him as he thought of them.

A second incident also took place in the countryside. He was travelling with three or four young Yugoslavs, visiting scattered Christians whom they knew in Serbia and other parts. Having drawn the car off the road for breakfast, they were somewhat alarmed at the sound of thundering hoofs, and the appearance of a cloud of dust, rapidly drawing near. Then over the brow of the hill they saw three or four horsemen driving a herd of cattle before them. The cattle passed by the parked vehicle and scattered to browse on the coarse grass, but the horsemen, two of them riding bare back, came galloping hard at the little group. It looked as though they intended to ride them down, but their horsemanship was superb. They brought their steeds to an abrupt halt within feet of the seated party, and turned out to be quite friendly teenagers. They exchanged greetings, asked where the travellers were from and where they were going, were obviously merely indifferently inquisitive, and suddenly wheeled their horses around and galloped off as abruptly as they had appeared. Ken's young companions went off to kick a football around, while he stretched himself out for a rest. Then he heard them shout, 'Ken! Ken! Watch!' so he sat up and looked in their direction.

'Not at us – watch him!' they called, and turning round he

saw that one of the horsemen had come up silently, on foot, and was standing staring down at him.

Ken saw that he was quite young, probably not more than fourteen years old, and asked smilingly, 'What's your name?'

'Yanche,' was the reply.

'Yanche – Johnnie,' repeated Ken, then asked if he could read.

'Yes' said the boy, and Ken drew a leaflet out of his bag. It was *The Way Of Salvation* in Serbian. Opening it, he pointed to some words and waited for the boy to read them. Slowly he did so.

'God loves the world so much He gave His only Son, that whoever believes in Him should not perish, but have everlasting life.'

Ken nodded encouragingly, and pointed to another.

'Believe in the Lord Jesus Christ and you will be saved . . .' He read that too, and looked at Ken questioningly. But there was no time for more. His companions reappeared, called him to come, and away he went.

But he had the little booklet in his pocket.

Almost certainly it was the only portion of the Word of God he had ever possessed – perhaps the only portion he ever would possess. In a Communist country there were millions of people who never would so much as hold a Bible in their hands, let alone be able to call one their own. Those few brief minutes might have been the only chance that young horseman would have in a lifetime to receive the news of the salvation extended to all mankind, as Ken very well knew. He was thankful he'd had that booklet handy, and that he had been sufficiently alert to pass it on, to take advantage of the fleeting opportunity.

It is a very solemn thing to have been put in trust with the Gospel.

He was travelling by car on another occasion in one of the countries of eastern Europe, when he saw a young soldier who thumbed a lift, so stopping he invited him in beside him.

As they drove along Ken tried to converse, but his knowledge of that particular language was too limited, and he had to give it up. There was one thing he could do, though. As he drove along his hand fumbled in the bag beside him, and he brought out a New Testament, and handed it to the man. He looked at it, saw what it was, kissed it, and then looked at Ken silently as he tucked it away inside his tunic. There was a significance about the way in which he did it that conveyed more to Ken than words could have done. They just looked at each other, their eyes meeting with a glance of understanding, then drove on silently. The New Testament was out of sight, but as the young soldier got out of the car with a word of thanks and a friendly gesture of farewell, Ken saw the bulge of a little book inside his tunic.

The bulge inside the tunic. There was something very telling about it. It spoke of a precious possession that had to be concealed for fear it would be snatched away, yet was of such value that any risk was worth taking to retain it.

He was to see that bulge many times in the years to come, as SGM booklets and leaflets arrived at the borders of lands where stern-faced officials looked with suspicion at anything that did not bear the imprint of their government's authority. He was to see some of those bundles of Scripture eagerly opened in the homes of his friends, then distributed carefully to those who would carry them over the borders.

Bulges in a suitcase, in a hold-all, in a shoulder-bag. Bulges even in the basket of a peasant woman, who was asked when she came to the border of the east European country where she lived, 'What have you got in that basket?'

'Bread for my family,' she answered promptly, and was waved on.

Ken was struck with the aptness of her reply when he heard of it. Bread for her family. 'Man does not live on bread alone, but on every word that comes from the mouth of God.'...It was his job to supply that bread.

6

Young Searchers in Africa

The decision to encourage staff members to go and see for themselves how and where SGM work could be forwarded overseas was not confined to the Area Secretaries, as Eric Cook was to discover. He was in charge of the young people's department, and conducted his work behind a door bearing the name of the Young Searchers League – YSL for short.

By the time he took it on it was a thriving department, but it had started away back in 1918 in a very casual manner, with a cheerful man who enjoyed cycling and who chatted with a group of children he found playing on a village green. He got into the habit of cycling out to see them once a week, and telling them Bible stories. But he had an unusual way of doing it – there was nothing dull or stereotyped about his method. Pulling a hand puppet out of his pocket, he pretended to be a ventriloquist, and held a conversation with it, asking questions about the Bible which the puppet answered. The children were enthralled. Sometimes they knew the answer before the puppet could get it out.

This led on to setting questions for them to answer themselves. At this point SGM began to get involved, for Ashley Baker helped to provide the questions – one to be answered in the words of Scripture from every chapter in the Gospel of John. The children who answered all the questions correctly got a prize, which provided a stimulus to the exercise. Then more questions were set, until the diligent had got through most of the Bible, and gained for themselves quite a library of awards.

The idea took on. Other groups of children were formed, and since they had to be given a name, they were called Young Searchers. They received a magazine, too, with Bible quizzes and stories, and news from other countries to widen their interests.

By 1966 there were several hundred groups of Young Searchers in the UK, and many 'Lone Searchers' who had no local group to which they could belong. But there was more to it than that. The movement had spread overseas, with missionaries who had known about it while still at home introducing it in areas to which they had gone. The question and answer method which demanded personal study of the Bible was one that could be used anywhere – and not only among children, either.

It had started in Sierra Leone, for instance, in a gaol. This is how it came about.

A Methodist missionary had gone, rather reluctantly, to visit a young prisoner who had sent a message urging her to come and see him. He had forged a cheque (very badly) while working in her office, and had landed himself in prison as a result. She wished the young culprit had chosen to address his plea to someone else.

She was already as busy as she thought she could be with the Girls' Brigade work she had started in Freetown, as well as the youth, social and women's work she was doing at the time. Furthermore, the prospect of going into the men's open prison was rather daunting. But she could not refuse the lad, so went along, to find he was just one of a group of other young men who gathered round as she talked to him, and begged her to come again and conduct a service for them. She realised that the request was prompted as much by desire for something to do as a genuine longing for religious teaching, but she agreed to go. The opportunity was too good to miss.

Then news of the services reached the closed prison, and

from there, too, came an urgent plea for her visits. Almost
before she knew it, she was so involved in prison work she
scarcely knew how to fit everything into her schedule. The
very emptiness of the prisoners' days provided a unique
opportunity to reach their minds, and then their consciences
and hearts, and she wondered how best to take advantage of
it.

It was at this point that she thought of the Young Searchers
League. The reading of a chapter of the Bible to find the right
answers to the set questions would give the men something to
do, and who could tell how such study would affect them
individually? She was already in touch with SGM headquarters in London, having obtained several grants of
Scriptures for use in her other work, so wrote asking for
further help, this time for YSL courses. She went on to
explain that they were not for children, but for men in prison.
Furthermore, she had to admit that in most cases they had no
Bibles. Was there any way in which Bibles could be obtained?
It was asking a lot, but...

She met with a prompt and sympathetic response. Not
only were the courses provided, but Bibles to go with them. 'I
was so grateful to the SGM,' she said years later, and
reflecting on the men who had gone through with the courses
(not all did so) she could report that none of them landed up
in gaol again. The Word of God had had its effect.

So the Young Searchers League was introduced in Sierra
Leone.

There was, of course, a different story to be told in all the
countries where it was established. By 1965 there were YSL
groups in a number of African countries, with touching
evidence of its effectiveness coming from time to time in
letters received from children like Amos, who wrote that he
had started the courses as a joke, but when he came to the
second verse in Daniel 12, which speaks of the resurrection, at
which some will awake to everlasting contempt and shame,
he had asked himself to which group he belonged, and

realised with alarm that it was to the latter group. 'From that time I decided to follow the Lord Jesus with all my being.'

Or like Nao who, coming to the last question in the course, which required her to say what effect it had had on her, stopped short and thought, 'I can't write anything truly – I haven't received the Lord Jesus.' Then and there she knelt down and on the basis of the words she had read in Revelation 3 verse 20, opened the door of her heart and asked Him to come in.

Eric Cook had been so inundated with correspondence from Africa and papers to be corrected, that he had sought and obtained outside help. One of his voluntary assistants had 10,000 enrolled members in Nigeria, and was receiving new applications at the rate of 500 each month. A telephone call to SGM one day announced that a letter box in Forest Hill, London (where she lived) was getting so jammed with letters that the postman was having difficulty in clearing it. The GPO therefore offered to send a van to collect the letters from her house – it would simplify matters to do it that way.

Even with the help of such volunteers as the lady in Forest Hill, Eric Cook was finding the flood of work coming into his department from Nigeria was more than he could cope with. The need for an office in the country itself became more and more evident. It was met when the Sudan Interior Mission (SIM), publishers of the magazine *African Challenge*, agreed to incorporate it in their own counselling department, with one of their own workers to oversee the work. This brought matters to a head. The leader of the Young Searchers League must go to Nigeria, not only to make the necessary arrangements with SIM, but to see for himself how best the study of the Bible through YSL's simple yet effective method could be extended. In spite of the unrest with the rebellion of the Biafrans against the central government in Lagos, the time seemed ripe for a move forward, not only in Nigeria, but in neighbouring Ghana as well.

So, early in January 1967 Eric Cook boarded a BOAC

plane at London Airport, bound for Lagos. He was to meet personally some of the people with whom he had been corresponding for years.

It was a heart-warming experience. Inevitably there was a welcome for him in missionary circles wherever he went. The camaraderie that exists between those who share a common faith is always intensified when they meet in a land not their own, to which they have gone for the common purpose of making that faith known. He had not been to West Africa before, but in the seven or eight weeks he was there, although he travelled thousands of miles, he was never without someone to make arrangements for him, meet him off planes or river-ferries to conduct him to the home where he was to stay, to introduce him to people needing the help his Mission could give, and to take him to often out of the way places he would never have found by himself.

One of those places was an African village where Wycliffe Bible Translators were at work among people of the Izi tribe. His department at home had a live link with them, for some of the elementary reading cards being prepared for use among the new literates were financed by the Young Searchers League. Now that he was on the spot, he could report back to them what he saw and heard, describe the villages in which the smiling, dark-skinned Izi people with their close-cropped curly black hair lived, and what it would mean to them to learn to read verses of Scripture in their own language. If the serenading by a group of young people dancing to the accompaniment of a six-piece band which wakened him one night at 1.30 a.m. could not be claimed as his best opportunity for personal evangelism, followed by the gift of a Scripture booklet, at any rate it provided a little local colour.

So did his description of a visit to a post office in a Nigerian town, where he walked along a dusty road with open drains on either side, to find himself in the midst of flocks of sheep or goats or both, all looking so alike he could not distinguish them from each other. He made good use of that when referring to the final judgment as portrayed in Matthew 24. People might outwardly look alike, but the Judge could distinguish between them, would know how to separate the sheep from the goats. Although the filming of a crocodile did not bring Scripture so readily to mind, he enjoyed doing it all the same. But what heartened him far more on that visit to Nigerian YSL groups and meetings held in schools was the eagerness of the children's response:

> Shared an evening service at Ochaja Secondary School and Teacher Training College. Twenty boys remained behind for counselling.
> Spoke at a YSL meeting in Ohena. A hundred and fifty boys attended out of a school of 400, despite the counter attraction of a film next door.
> Visited Titcombe YSL Centre, which is experiencing difficulty because of the large numbers wishing to participate. [That sort of difficulty was welcome.]

It was touching to go with the representative of the Nigerian Bible Society to a government school for the blind. 'This school is run by Roman Catholic nuns, who had received Braille Scriptures from SGM, and were most enthusiastic about them. A number of the young people will be shortly commencing the YSL questions in Braille, sending their answers to the Torch Trust for the Blind, in Crawley, Sussex.'

The visit to Nigeria resulted, among other things, in the formation of at least eight new YSL groups, and three more among the blind. And it gave him an insight into the ways in which SGM literature was being used. One of the highlights of his trip was to arrive at a training centre for young evangelists on the very morning when they were being instructed in the use of the familiar little leaflet *Four Things God Wants You to Know*. It had been produced in their own language, which of course he did not know, but he knew its contents by heart, and realised that those twenty young men were receiving intensive tuition on the personal application before fanning out, far and wide, to pass it on to others.

This, he thought appreciatively, was the correct way in which SGM books and leaflets should be used – not in indiscriminate distribution, but selectively. It was encouraging to see how this method was being instilled into the minds of young Christians in this rather remote area of West Africa. And again, attending an open air meeting in another place, he noticed *New Life in Christ*, this time in the Igala language, being used in private conversations with people who had been listening on the outskirts of the crowd. He would have something to tell Ken Andrewartha and his colleagues in the Translations Department back in London, when he got home. It was quite exciting to see those little booklets with which he was so familiar in English, making their appearance in a variety of translations right here in African villages, and being received with such eagerness.

He also observed that leaflets with a patterned design rather than a pictorial one, were more acceptable. Pictures that were suitable in one country were quite bewildering in another. That was something to report back to the Production Department. Although he had gone to West Africa primarily in connection with his own department, YSL, he kept his eye open for anything that would affect others. And at certain stages of his tour he went as representative of another department altogether.

A recent change in government in Ghana had resulted in much greater freedom for Christians, and it was to Ghana that he went as representative of the organisation within SGM that concentrated on reaching members of the armed forces. Here he was plunged into entirely different circles, and some very exhilarating experiences.

He was met at the airport at Accra, not by a Western missionary in an open-necked shirt who had just driven up in a jeep, but by a smartly dressed African in military uniform who had a limousine, chauffeur-driven, waiting for him. He was the senior chaplain, the Rev Major J. Kweku-Kyereboah, and he had come to escort Mr Eric Cook to the Burma Camp, headquarters of the Armed Forces of Ghana. So in Ghana his first conversations were not with fellow-Westerners, but with Ghanaian senior officers, and although arrangements had been made for him to attend to YSL affairs during the afternoon, the reception he attended in the evening was in the home of the Roman Catholic chaplain, and held for chaplains and senior officers of Burma Camp.

It was all very different from visiting schools, speaking to children, and seeing missionaries at work in the bush. He was, as the saying goes, wearing a different hat now. He had come at a time of exceptional opportunity, for the National Liberation Council, now in control, actually encouraged the propagation of Christianity. SGM had been quick to enter an open door, and had made arrangements for the production of Bibles and New Testaments bearing the crest of the Ghanaian Armed Forces, and at the chaplain's reception these were displayed.

'Considerable interest was shown in these,' Eric wrote, 'as there was also in SGM portions, especially the Easter booklet. Requests were immediately made for supplies of these to be sent, and in order to expedite delivery the Army Commander offered to send the order by teleprinter to the Ghanian Embassy in London. It was therefore suggested that supplies should be delivered to the Embassy so that part, at least, could be delivered through the diplomatic bag.'

Things had got off to a good start, and more was to follow. An army staff car for his journeys, complete with chauffeur and an official army photographer, was put at his disposal. And as the senior chaplain, with whom he was soon on a Christian-names footing, accompanied him on all his journeys, a firm friendship was formed between them which persisted long after Eric had returned to England.

During his stay in Ghana he travelled 1,500 miles, visited schools and colleges, mission centres and army barracks, a leprosarium and a studio where recordings were made for broadcasts through ELWA, a Christian radio station.

In this variety of experiences it was inspiring to see the encouragement given by men in key positions. Reporting on a meeting he addressed to the officers and men in the garrison chapel at Takoradi, he wrote:

> The Roman Catholic chaplain was particularly keen to see the RSV Bible which, of course, is not acceptable to his Church. He followed my address by strongly commending the reading of the Scripture, and requested any who wanted to purchase Bibles to give their names in at his office. Immediately following this address there was a queue of some forty men wishing to make application for Bibles.

Back in Burma Camp arrangements were made for Bibles to be presented to all the members of the National Liberation Council, and he was personally conducted to present a specially crested Bible to the Chairman of the Council.

That concluded his involvement with the Ghanaian Army and its chaplains. His days of having a chauffeur-driven car at his disposal were at an end. He had enjoyed the experience while it lasted. Now he went off to stay in the home of a missionary, and help to sell Bibles at one of the stalls at the Industrial Trade Fair, where he may be said to have reverted to his original position as leader of the Young Searchers League. It was all in a day's work!

A couple of days later he returned to Nigeria, and then back to England to present his report. His mission had been accomplished. The transfer of YSL centres in Nigeria to the Niger Challenge Publications in Lagos had been satisfactorily arranged, with a suitable link-up in Ghana, and a number of new YSL centres had been established in both countries.

But he had another report to present as well. It was in

connection with those visits made to the chaplains and senior officers of Burma Camp, headquarters of the Ghanaian Armed Forces. He had gone as the accredited representative of an organisation known to them as the Naval, Military and Air Force Bible Society. It was housed in an office opposite his own on the first floor of SGM, so he had no difficulty in giving an uninhibited, verbal account to his colleague there of all that had happened.

It was all very informal, accompanied by a cup of coffee. It was part of the continuing history of a little society started nearly two hundred years before, and which had been associated with SGM since 1910.

But that is another story, and must be related in another chapter.

7

In the Prayer Department

The door of the editorial office closed with a sharp click, and
Winifred Marden returned to her desk hoping that she would
be left undisturbed for at least an hour. Or two. Or for the rest
of the day, although she knew that was too much to expect.
All the same, she needed the time. The completed copy of the
next issue of *News Digest* ought to be in hand and ready for
the printers by 6 p.m., and as usual there were last minute
selections to be made from the mass of material that had
accumulated since she had prepared the previous issue. And
as soon as that was off, there would be the Prayer Fellowship
leaflet to produce. In her capacity as Editor it was her task to
keep SGM friends and supporters aware of what was
happening, so on her desk arrived all the news, making her
office a sort of hub and centre of information to which letters
and reports found their way from all over the world. In
addition to what came to her through SGM sources, about
200 missionary magazines were received each month, quite
apart from all the news that came through secular channels.
Then it was up to her to select, interpret and summarise it all,
and present it in a succinct and readable form, to stimulate
and encourage prayer.

It was a job that put her on her mettle. Her senior
colleagues, she realised almost with surprise, depended on
her for accurate information. And when she learned that
items mentioned in the Prayer Fellowship leaflet were liable

to be broadcast over a number of foreign radio stations, she was almost alarmed at the responsibility she was shouldering. She sometimes wondered how it had come about, and looked back with a smile to the day when she had first arrived, as a very junior typist, and had been quite awe-struck at what she found.

The first thing that had struck her was that the place was so clean. No cigarette ends, no bits of paper dropped carelessly on the floor. No smell of smoke, or cheap perfume, no whiff, here and there, of alcohol. It was evidently swept, cleaned and dusted every day, although glancing round as she left for home that evening she wondered what the cleaners had to do.

And it was efficiently run. She was really surprised that what she had thought of as a little-known Christian organisation like SGM, housed in an old-fashioned Victorian building with deep-set windows and stone stairs, should have such good quality equipment and high standards of production. She wondered if her own work would measure up.

The third thing about it that impressed her was that the men were so polite to the women. They even opened the door and stood back for her to go in ahead of them! And every day started with a prayer meeting...

Altogether, it was all very different from the government office where she had been working previously.

It had been a surprise, too, when two or three years later Ashley Baker had called her into his office and told her he wanted her to take on the editorial work. 'But I've no training...! No experience...!' But Ashley Baker had been confident he was making the right appointment, assured her that the Lord would help her, and in the course of a long conversation gave her a bit of advice she never forgot.

'You need to know where to find your *reliable* information.'

'How right he was!' she said many years later. 'In the Editorial Department we are blessed in having a row of reference books in front of us, and along the corridor many long-suffering colleagues who will share their knowledge with us and let us borrow their files.' She got into the habit of going along to check any bit of information that came her way with one of her colleagues who would know more about it than she. There were many pitfalls to avoid in the presentation of news, she found.

There was the occasion, for instance, when she inserted an interesting little item to the effect that for the very first time a Christian radio programme was going out in a certain South American republic. When the item appeared in print Mighell Smith had a word with her about it.

'Where did you get that bit of information?' he asked. She showed him the report in one of the hundred and more missionary magazines that had come to her that month. He looked at it, then said wryly, 'As a matter of fact, there are two other missionary societies working in that area, and they've been broadcasting for about ten years.' She gasped with dismay, and he added comfortingly, 'I suppose this society either didn't know what the others were doing, or meant that this was the first time they had produced a Christian radio programme. Alas! – we can't afford to take everything at face value!'

She had been more cautious about accepting everything she saw in print after that. And there had been an even more disturbing incident, following a private bit of news that came her way. It was about an Englishman working with Iraqi Airways, living in Baghdad, who was having Bible studies with two or three Iraqi friends who came to his house from time to time. There would have been nothing unusual about it if it had happened in a country where there was religious freedom, but coming from a Muslim state, it was news. She decided to insert a small paragraph, carefully worded, to the effect that an English businessman in Iraq was studying the Bible with two or three neighbours, in his own home.

Some time later an urgent request came from the Englishman himself, requesting that they never refer to such matters again. The police, having been appraised of the article, had traced the story to its source, called at his home and questioned him for a long time.

News Digest evidently travelled far beyond the friends and supporters of SGM for whom it was produced, even appearing on the desks of embassies and government offices.

Winifred was alarmed. Her natural desire, as an editor, for items of unusual news, had put someone at risk, and might even have hindered the very thing for which SGM existed – the spread of the Word of God where it was most needed. The experience put her on her guard, and made her very cautious about divulging anything that might lead to hostile questioning. So she was very cautious about letting it be known that a senior staff member of SGM had gone to Afghanistan.

Afghanistan! The very name smacked of danger and intrigue, of rocky plains and barren mountains over which wild horsemen and fanatical Muslims swept with swords and knives unsheathed, the terror of any who were foolhardy enough to venture on their territory. It conjured up pictures of the North-West Frontier and the Khyber Pass, of sinister Russian secret agents and naïve British soldiers, caught up like pawns in a political game they did not understand. And, as everybody knew, Afghanistan was a land closed to the Christian message. There was no doubt about that. The whole Bible had been translated into Farsi, and was easily obtainable in the neighbour state of Iran, but anyone bringing a copy over the border did so at his own risk.

In fact, if anyone was looking for martyrdom, the swift way to achieve it would be to go to Afghanistan and start proclaiming Jesus Christ as the Son of God.

It is true that by the time the senior staff member of SGM went there a well-qualified team of Christian doctors, nurses and other specialists from the West was working in the country, under the leadership of Dr Christy Wilson. They met for worship together in a house quite openly. Reluctant

permission had been granted for that. Their services in a
country where 10 per cent of the population suffered from
glaucoma were too valuable to lose, even on religious
grounds. The Christians from the West must be allowed to
worship their Christ, and even invite others to their meetings.
But the time soon came when no Afghan might join them. To
do so would be courting almost certain imprisonment, if not
death.

It was a delicate situation for Christy Wilson and his team.
Here were the people of Afghanistan, millions of them,
without any knowledge that Jesus Christ, through His death,
had opened for them the door to everlasting life. Yet officially
the lips of the members of the team were sealed. All they
could do, it seemed, was to pray and wait for the day when
Christ might be proclaimed to these friendly, hospitable
people among whom they lived.

However, waiting and praying revealed that there was
something else that they could do. They could plan. That is
why the SGM man was in Kabul for a visit in 1966. The team
wanted to be prepared for the day when the Word of God
could be freely distributed among Afghans, and there was
one group of Afghans, numbering about five millions, in
whose particular tongue was not one portion of the Word of
God. That group spoke Dari, the Afghan form of Farsi.

When the SGM man returned from his visit to Afghanistan, he had several consultations in the Translations
Department about getting something produced in Dari. Then
followed some correspondence between the leader of the
team in Kabul and the Translations Department of SGM,
where a file was opened containing a progress report for:

  Language: DARI; Afghan.
  Country: Afghanistan.

Winifred knew enough about it to realise that it was
something of major importance, and sufficiently picturesque

to capture the interest, too. But as it had been emphasised that 'every care must still be taken not to publicise what is going on' she knew she could do nothing but refer very obliquely to anything connected with Afghanistan.

There were so many things to take into account when providing what was known as 'fuel for prayer'. The main purpose in producing *News Digest* and *Prayer Fellowship* leaflets was to stimulate and encourage believing intercession, for without it the Mission would soon subside, like a balloon that was being deflated. If people did not receive information, how would they know what to pray for, and how would their interest be maintained? On the other hand, if the information got into the wrong hands irreparable harm might be done. She weighed it up, decided that the risk was too great. She must keep quiet about hopes that something would be produced in Dari. Prayer for the translation of suitable Scriptures into the language was mainly confined to the meetings for staff alone, held each day at SGM headquarters. Perhaps the very fact that it had to be kept secret added earnestness and intensity to the prayers of those who knew what was involved.

Winifred, as the one responsible for compiling prayer requests, was informed of what was going on in the Translations Department. They hoped to produce an initial booklet in Dari containing selections from the Psalms and Proverbs, if someone with an adequate knowledge of the language could be found to prepare it. They would be sending out a supply of good paper to Kabul, on which the calligrapher could do the work, then it could be photographed. There was the suggestion that the first edition should have 10,000 copies printed.

There were various fine points to be considered, such as the title. The Translations Department, in a letter to Dr Christy Wilson, suggested that 'Proverbs and Psalms' might be more acceptable than vice versa. In his reply he thanked them for the idea, but thought that, not only for chronological reasons, but because David was more respected than Solomon, it would be better to stick to 'Psalms and Proverbs'. All these things had to be taken into consideration. So the correspondence continued backwards and forwards and away there in Kabul things were looking very hopeful. For the first time in known history a Christian church was being built. True, it was for expatriates, not for Afghans, but it would be a witness to Christ right there in the heart of that Muslim country. The time would surely come when the Gospel could be proclaimed, and the Word of God distributed among the people themselves. And as the Afghans had nothing in their own language something must be ready for them.

Then came a dramatic reverse, and a turn of events in Afghanistan itself, that brought the whole project to a halt. By royal edict the newly built church was pulled down. The tall, modern building that had been seen so clearly visible especially from the planes that flew over the city, was reduced to a pile of timber and rubble.

But that was not the end. The day after the last lorry load of rubble had been removed a revolution within the country resulted in a political coup and the overthrow of a dynasty that had reigned for over 200 years.

The promptness with which it happened was significant, and there were those among the Afghans who murmured, 'Is the Christian's God angry that His building has been destroyed? Is that why the King has been overthrown?' Perhaps the Christian's God would have to be reckoned with by the new government? Perhaps it would do something to placate Him. However, the new government did not take that view. If anything, the Christian medical team had to be more careful than ever. In the general upheaval, the matter of a production in Dari lapsed.

The file on Dari in the Translations Department of SGM was closed. Nothing of importance was added to it for about eight years. It remained a topic of prayer, though it could not be transferred to the praise file – not yet.

Then there was the matter of a booklet for the Tuaregs, the veiled men of the Sahara. A file had been opened dealing with their language, Tamajeq, in 1938. Later, a missionary working in their neighbourhood had been eager for something to be produced for them, and had done her best, but the Translations Department, having eventually found someone with an adequate knowledge of the language to check the manuscript received, learned that there were serious flaws in the translation. Among other items, the word that had been chosen for 'prayer', like the scorpion, had a sting in its tail. It meant 'a prayer with a curse'.

That file was closed, too. It remained closed for years. But it stayed open in the prayer department.

Meanwhile, there was plenty going on that could be reported with confidence. Eric Cook's visit to Nigeria and Ghana provided a fund of encouraging material, while from Indonesia were coming demands for the Scriptures that far exceeded the supplies.

'If only you knew how bare our shelves are now!' came word from a Bible Institute in Java. 'We gave all our available supplies to our eighteen teams of students, and they will be gone for nearly three months.' Some of those teams went into the jungle of Sumatra, and sent back enthusiastic reports of meetings held from early afternoon until late in the night, with the exhausted preachers being kept awake with the earnest pleas, 'Oh, brother, don't stop yet. We know so little. Please open that book and read some more.'

From one area came news of 200 people who, having received and read quite small SGM leaflets, met regularly for prayer and worship, and from another that 300 people had professed faith in Christ. There were more personal and intimate glimpses, too, from time to time, of individuals being reached. One missionary wrote of waiting at the crossroads for a bus and getting into conversation with an elderly man who was also waiting there. The man was friendly, and as he showed interest, the missionary produced what was his last copy of *Good News*, and gave it go him.

Some time later the missionary heard that there was an old man in a certain village who had a book called *Good News*, and was often seen reading it, so he went in search of him. Sure enough, it was the man he had met at the crossroads. The old man was glad to see him, and welcomed him whenever he arrived for a visit, and one day he said, 'You know, it is not you who have been searching for me – it's God,' and holding up *Good News* he went on to say, 'I've read and re-read this book, and now I understand that only Jesus Christ is Lord.'

Stories like that had an elating result and a subduing one. The elating result was satisfaction at the effectiveness of the Word of God on that old Indonesian man, as he read it thoughtfully and with an open mind. The subduing effect was less obvious, but perhaps more challenging. The missionary had said that the copy of *Good News* he had given the old man was the last one he possessed. The grant of Scriptures he had received from SGM had run out. Like the Bible Institute in Java, the shelves were bare, and the question arose – when could they be re-filled? The question arose over and over again.

One of the perennial problems of those in SGM responsible for the allocation of funds was to decide how and where to spend the money entrusted to them. Since adopting the method of making their requests known only to God, they had never run into debt, but there had been times when they realised with dismay that they were sailing very close to the wind. Now another difficulty was arising. With country after country emerging from colonial rule to independence there came changes in orthography and scripts which presented them with the alarming prospect of wasted stock. When new governments insisted on certain languages being dropped, the publications in those languages that had been so carefully, and in some cases, so expensively produced, would be useless. Caution in the expenditure of money, which was rarely in lavish supply anyway, meant that there were occasions when urgent needs could not be met.

The preciousness of the Word of God, so easily obtainable in her own country, was brought home forcibly to Winifred as she read the letters and reports that came from lands where all too often there was a dearth of it. There was a story from Africa of a man who travelled a very long distance to obtain supplies of two of the SGM booklets that had been produced in the Tshiluba language. He was a teacher and an earnest Christian, but had no textbooks from which to teach Scripture. These booklets would fulfil that purpose, and he wanted them so that the children could study what the Bible taught for themselves. 'And they will also read them aloud in their villages,' he assured the bookshop manager to whom he had come, and asked for 150 copies of each booklet. But the bookshop manager could only supply him with fifty. Deeply dispirited, he returned home with only one third of what he had hoped to obtain. Winifred was constantly receiving reports like that. The booklets were excellent, the translation splendid, but they were not enough to meet the need.

However, there was a bright side to the picture, too. An evangelist in Ethiopia was approached one day by a man who asked, 'Could you please repair this little book for me?' He held out what looked like a dog-eared, tattered bundle of paper, so worn that the evangelist did not at first recognise it. Then he saw it was the SGM booklet *God Has Spoken* in the Tigrinya language.

The evangelist took it from the man, looked at it, shook his head and said, 'I'm afraid it's past repairing. It won't last much longer.'

The man's disappointment was obvious, and the evangelist, with a smile, opened his satchel and drew out a brand new booklet bearing the same title as the old one.

'Would you like a new copy instead?'

Stories like that, which came to her quite frequently, were

heart-warming and encouraging, and she was glad to pass them on, but they also contained a veiled reproach. These people treasured their own little booklet, the only portion they had of the Word of God. How different things were for her. She had a row of Bibles and New Testaments of her own, in various translations, some with Bible studies, some with appendices, some with marginal cross references, and she knew where she could go and buy a new one whenever she wanted it. The same applied to many of the people to whom *News Digest* and the Prayer Fellowship leaflet would come. Would they, too, be reminded of the challenging words, 'From everyone who has been given much, much will be demanded!'

The principle of moving men's hearts through God, by prayer, was constantly referred to in the private prayer meetings held at SGM each day. And it was not confined to money, either. A recurring need was that of suitable staff. In 1963, the year when John Kennedy, President of the USA was assassinated, the SGM was faced with an acute need in India. There had been difficulties with some of the Indian staff, notably the young Punjabi who had been Mrs Junkison's right-hand man for years. He had left the work, and now that her retirement (and that of Dr Western) was already overdue, the need for a successor was urgent. But no one was forthcoming. Eventually a Finnish missionary agreed to be responsible for the administration, but made it quite plain she could not undertake the travelling to conferences all over India that was required for the development of the work.

The staff need in India was a matter of urgent prayer at HQ in London, and it took quite a time for the Lord's provision to be made evident. As sometimes happens, the provision was right on the spot, but no one saw it at first. Perhaps it was a case, not so much for them waiting for God as of God waiting for them to see what he had prepared. There were various consultations held in London and Bangalore, and correspondence between the two centres before the name of Joe Carroll came up. Then things began to fall into place. The very man for the job became evident. Joe had British blood in his veins, but he was basically an Indian. He knew India and the Indians better than any Westerner, was strong and unattached, would be free to go off at a moment's notice, if necessary, and the crowded stations and long train journeys would hold no fear for him.

Furthermore, his heart was in SGM. He had proved that, working steadily as a packer in the warehouse in Clapham for years, where his varied gifts as a speaker and a communicator had little opportunity for expression.

The prayer request that had been on the file for some weeks was transferred to the praise list when it became known that Joe Carroll was to go to help in the SGM office in Bangalore.

8

Joe Again

On his arrival in India Joe found he had to fill a bigger gap than he had expected. The difficulties with the Indian staff had resulted in the loss of all the experienced workers, and he had to start training new ones. Then the Finnish missionary's health broke down, and she had to retire, and there was no one but Joe to take her place. Almost before he knew where he was, he found himself in charge of the printing, packing and distribution of SGM literature to places all over India, with all the correspondence, telephone calls, visitors, that were involved and with only an untrained staff to help him. It was all very different from the packing of parcels that had occupied most of his working hours in London. But at any rate he was in his own well planned city of Bangalore, with its wide, modern streets, its open markets and dusty lanes tucked behind them, its throngs of men in their loose fitting cotton garments and women in their fluttering saris, its limousines and its horse-drawn carts, its wayside stalls and its beggars, its holy men and its sacred cows. The sights and the sounds and the smells were all familiar to him. He was in his own country and city and he was at home there.

It was well that it was so. The background of his life presented no problems in the matter of daily living, for he adapted back without difficulty to the food and the climate, and could devote his whole attention to the task on hand. He hurried along each morning to turn off from the busy street into the peaceful, secluded compound where the office was still situated in time to receive from the postman the bundle of letters that were delivered daily – orders for literature, requests for samples, donations, printers' queries, bills, specimens of paper, and invitations to attend conferences in churches of all denominations in all parts of India. Then they all had to be dealt with, duties assigned, arrangements made. His days were so full he had no time to develop a private, social life for himself – but he thrived on the very thing that would have proved too much for many men. He was busy from morning till night, answering letters and telephone calls, receiving visitors, overseeing the execution of orders and the keeping of accounts, then preparing exhibitions for a conference that might involve him in travelling all night as well as all day to some distant part of India.

He enjoyed the travelling. If it was tiring and uncomfortable, sitting for hours on end in a train that chugged its way across the plains, stopping at stations where the food vendors swarmed up and down the platforms and passengers scrambled in and out, shouting for porters, it provided him with so many opportunities to talk to strangers he would otherwise never have met, that it was well worth it. The bundle of leaflets and booklets he carried with him was reduced steadily in size on every journey he took, while page after page of his notebook was filled with new names and addresses of people he would follow up later. And when he arrived at his destination, he never knew what would be expected of him – whether to preach at a moment's notice, or go off with a bag of booklets to a village a few miles away, or to listen to a discussion lasting hours between church elders about some local problem.

One of those journeys took him to Rajasthan, a vast and barren province bordering on Pakistan. He had gone at the invitation of the Indian principal of a Bible School that ran correspondence courses in which SGM booklets were used. But the principal was not satisfied.

'We've got these courses in Hindi, and they are good,' he told Joe. 'They are reaching all sorts of men. But what about the women? Haven't you got anything for women? We need something for women.'

It set Joe thinking. The women of India. He knew something of the lives so many of them lived; hard-working, bearing children, drudges in the fields as well as in the home if they were poor; or idle, bearing children, shut up in their compounds and deprived of freedom if they were rich. Accustomed as they were to believing themselves inferior in every way to men, even those with an elementary knowledge of the Gospel were unaware of their worth in the eyes of God. The principal of the Bible School had highlighted a need that he felt SGM should be meeting, and Joe made note of it.

A booklet for the women of India – that was what was needed. Something to make them realise the dignity God had bestowed on them when His Son was born into the world through a human mother. Something that would reveal His compassion towards such as the woman taken in adultery, or the widow whose only son had died. Something that would indicate the part that women had played as followers of Jesus, the privilege accorded to one of them to be the first disciple to see Him alive after His resurrection...

He thought a lot about it, then wrote to London. So started the consultations and Bible searching and careful compilation of what eventually came into being with the title *God's Message To Women*. It took years to complete – the booklets were gone over and over again before they were finally printed, and this one had to be translated into Hindi, a major national language of India. But it was delivered at last, and then it was advertised over the radio, so that hundreds of letters began arriving at the correspondence-course office, almost more than they could cope with. And then the Good News Broadcasting Company decided to include it in their follow-up programme. It became a regular piece of SGM stock, constantly being reprinted, and by the end of 1986 had been translated into six other languages as well.

But it all started when the principal of the Bible School in Rajasthan had challenged Joe by asking 'Haven't you got anything for the women of India?'

How widely effective the booklet proved to be in individual lives, of course, there was no means of assessing, any more than with any other piece of literature. Like most of the members of SGM staff, Joe turned frequently to the promise in Isaiah's prophecy that God's Word would not return void, but would accomplish what God had sent it to do, and left it at that. But there were times when the curtain veiling its accomplishment was drawn aside, and one occasion remained vividly etched on his memory in connection with one of the oldest and most widely distributed of all the booklets.

He was in his office-cum-showroom in Bangalore one day when, looking round, he saw standing in the doorway an old man, peering short-sightedly into the room. His shirt and trousers were crumpled and rather grubby, his slippers flopped loosely on his feet. He seemed hesitant, so Joe said encouragingly,

'Come in. Can I help you?'

The old man entered the room and slowly drew something out of his pocket. It was a little book, so tattered and dirty with handling that Joe did not recognise it.

'I want a new one,' said the old man simply, and Joe saw that he was holding a copy of *Daily Strength*, in Urdu.

'Certainly,' he said. 'I'll get you one now,' and coming back with a new copy handed it to his visitor. The old man took it cautiously, still clutching his old copy, and held it up close to his eyes to examine it. Then his face broke into a smile.

'It's the same!' he exclaimed delightedly, clapping his hands together. Then he held out the old copy to Joe, saying,

'You can have this.'

Joe looked at it curiously, then asked, 'When did you get this?'

'A mem-sahib gave it to me,' replied the old man. 'I was on a train, and a Western woman, a mem-sahib, was in the carriage, and she gave it to me. I can't see very well, but I saw it was in my own language, so I read it. The type was big enough for me to see. Then I read it again, and I kept on reading it.' He lowered his voice, and looking at Joe said, 'And I believed what it said.'

He hesitated a moment, then continued in the same low voice. 'I believe in the Lord now. But you know what this country is. I'm a Muslim, and I daren't let them know.' Although he was employed as gatekeeper to a Roman Catholic convent, it was of his Muslim family and neighbours he was afraid. 'But I believe in the Lord in my heart.'

'Come back in two or three days' time, and I will give you another book that you can read,' Joe promised him, and four days later the old man turned up. 'Here's the book I promised you,' said Joe holding out a New Testament, explaining what it was. The old man touched his forehead, then bent down and touched Joe's feet in a gesture of gratitude, took the New Testament, and went away with it carefully concealed inside his shirt. Joe never saw him again.

A few months later he was again in the office when a white-robed figure entered, and Joe saw she was an Indian Roman Catholic nun. She looked round her in a rather supercilious manner, and when Joe asked if he could help her, replied that she wanted to know a little more about the place.

'Who are you? What do you do? How long have you been here?' she wanted to know. Joe explained that SGM was an organisation that gave away booklets containing words of Scripture – nothing else. It was not connected with any denomination, Protestant or Roman Catholic. It existed merely to distribute the Word of God, so was suitable for anyone to use and read. She picked up a few booklets, glanced through them, then said she would like to have a supply.

'Perhaps I ought to explain that we don't give them away to

anyone who comes and asks for them,' said Joe. 'They are only supplied to people who know what they are distributing, and undertake to use them wisely. For instance, here is a little booklet specially prepared for Muslims... here is one for people who are in sorrow... here is one for people who are trying to find out the truth... and so on. So the distributor has to know, to some extent, the contents of the booklet, and personally have confidence in it. They are not for indiscriminate distribution.' He spoke courteously enough, and the nun listened and nodded her head.

'I am the Mother Superior of the convent near here,' she said. 'And my old gatekeeper has had a copy of the New Testament given him – he told me you provided it. I've noticed a change in him since he's had this book. I feel it would be useful to have a supply of your literature.' So Joe gave her a supply of booklets and leaflets in four different languages of India, and off she went with them. He never saw her again, either.

There was a lapse of several more months before the story was taken up, this time by the arrival of another nun who did not hesitate to explain who she was and what she wanted.

'I come from Bombay,' she said. 'I've been on tour, and the Mother Superior of the convent near here showed me some of your booklets and advised me to come and see you. I should like to have a supply for distribution.' Again Joe pointed out that the literature was supplied only on the understanding that it would be distributed with discrimination, backed by prayer. The nun nodded approvingly, and promising to abide by these conditions departed with a bundle of booklets in her bag.

Although he never saw her again, he did not lose contact with her, for some weeks later she wrote to him, asking if he would be prepared to send, at her own expense, SGM booklets to a list of places that she would supply. She enclosed a gift for the work. Joe replied that he would certainly do as she asked, on the understanding that these booklets also should be given away personally, to meet a conscious need. Yes, she assured him, this should be done. As she visited various Roman Catholic institutions, schools, clinics, dispensaries, hospitals, she would instruct people in the use of the booklets. So the booklets were duly packed and despatched to the list of addresses that she supplied. And as Joe saw them being taken off to the Post Office, he glowed with the realisation that those booklets would find their way into the hands of innumerable people who would probably have refused to accept them at his hands when they knew he was not a Roman Catholic.

And he wondered who that unknown mem-sahib was who had given that copy of *Daily Strength* to a stranger on a train, years ago...

Joe remained in India for over three years before Bhakia Raj was found to take charge of the work there. When he returned to SGM in London it was no longer as a warehouse worker. He was asked to take on the job of Area Secretary for South Asia, the Middle East and North Africa. This involved promoting the production and distribution of SGM booklets in that vast area, and being on the alert to recognise where the needs and the opportunities were the greatest.

The office allocated to him for the pursuance of this task was about six feet wide and nine feet long, contained three steel filing cabinets, a desk, typewriter, two chairs, a telephone, and a waste paper basket. On one wall was a large map of the area of his responsibility, while the other provided the space for various notes, information and reminders to be hung up from time to time.

This little office, with its window providing a view of the traffic, stopping and starting at the Buckingham Palace Road crossing, became the centre of all his activities. Here he arrived first thing in the morning to sort out his mail and prepare to give a brief report when it was his turn to give news of his area at the 9 a.m. prayer meeting, and here he remained for the rest of the day unless he had some appointment to keep or meeting to attend. (He made a point of attending the annual meetings of all the missionary societies working in his area.) He had learned to type quite quickly, yet his pile of correspondence never seemed to be completely cleared, for the telephone, that relentless invader, broke in time and time again to interrupt him.

'I'm phoning from Heathrow. Passing through London... thought it would be an opportunity to get in touch with you about another supply of *The Way Of Salvation* for that Central Asian tribe I told you about...'

'Can I come and see you? I'll be in London for a couple of days, en route for Pakistan...'

'Meester Car-roll? Meester Car-roll? I get your letter in my country. Now I in your country. I want come and see you. How I get to your place...?'

Often enough it was the receptionist phoning from the showroom downstairs to tell him someone had arrived to see him, and down the stairs he would speed to greet the visitor and escort him up to his office. Sometimes it was a missionary seeking information about available booklets for his particular field, sometimes an enterprising young student wanting leaflets in other languages for distribution among overseas students in his college, sometimes a clergyman concerned about the Asian immigrants in his parish. And rarely a week passed without a visitor arriving from one of the countries of South Asia, or the Middle East, or North Africa.

A pastor from Egypt, with news of what was going on in the villages.

An evangelist from Sri Lanka, full of what was happening in the prisons there.

A believer from Iraq, burdened with the needs and difficulties of Christian witness in his country.

When the visitor had come for the first time, Joe escorted him on a tour of Radstock House. He always started at the prayer room, at the end of the long corridor.

'This is the heart of the Mission,' he told his visitor. 'It is part of our reference library. Look at all these shelves,' pointing to the long bookcase stretching along one wall. 'What is on these? Nothing but the Word of God. All of these are Bibles and New Testaments in different languages – over 400 of them. Look, here is the Bible in your language,' sliding open the glass door to extract a volume and hand it to his visitor to look at.

'And we are regularly producing booklets like those you use – and a lot more, too – in nearly all these languages. Our booklets and leaflets contain nothing but the Word of God.

'And you see that map?' pointing to the huge map of the world over the platform at the end of the room. 'We pray for the people in every part of the world twice a year. We pray for you, here in this room, twice a year.'

'Pray for us – here?'

'Yes. Look at this Prayer Remembrancer. You see this list of countries and areas – every part of the world is listed here, under the continents. Let's look at Africa:

First Day – Morocco
Second day – Algeria
Third day – Tunisia and Libya
Fourth Day – United Arab Republic (Egypt)

'On the fourth day of May and the fourth day of November we pray for Egypt ... And because I know you, we shall pray for *you*, and your work for the Lord...'

Joe had the Prayer Remembrancer at his fingertips, and knew just where to point to focus the attention of each individual visitor. He sometimes noticed tears in their eyes, especially those who came from lonely and discouraging situations, and paused for a minute before continuing, 'This is the heart of the Mission – prayer, and the Word of God.'

Then the tour continued, back along the corridor, pausing

at this door or that door with a word of explanation, 'Here is the Production Department, where the artists are at work, and where the format of each booklet is planned. It has to differ from country to country, to suit national tastes and prejudices. In some places a picture on the cover will appeal – in some places it will deter. Colour, too. Take *The Way Of Salvation*, for instance. For years, for as long as I can remember, it has been produced with a red cover. We used to call it the little red book. But when Mao Tse-tung, in China, produced *The Thoughts of Mao Tse-tung*, and had them printed in a little book with a red cover, we had to change the colour in some countries. In the Middle East, for instance, people thought we were distributing Mao Tse-tung's thoughts! So we had to be careful to produce it in green for Syria and Saudi Arabia, and other Middle East countries.

'That's why it's so important for us to get to know people like you – you can tell us what is acceptable and what isn't, in the place where you come from. Come in and have a word with the Production Manager...'

And so on along the corridor, pointing out the Translation Department, the Editorial Department, Young Searchers' League, Area Secretary for Africa, Area Secretary for the Far East, Area Secretary for Europe, and so on.

The tour that started in the prayer room always ended up in the stock room on the ground floor, with its corridors of shelves, rows and rows of them, stacked with Bibles, New Testaments, Gospels, booklets and leaflets. As Joe conducted his visitor through this department, he waxed eloquent, for there was something about it that stirred him, as he saw the packers at work, carefully sorting and packing the bundles that were to be addressed, weighed, stamped, and taken off to the Post Office that very day.

'The Word of God, going out all over the world from this place!'

The tour was over, but not the visit. When a visitor from overseas came to see an Area Secretary, the tour of the building always ended up in his or her office.

'Now we'll have a cup of tea and a talk, and see what we can
do to help you. What leaflets you need – any suggestions you
have to make about their appearance . . . And before you go,
let us pray together . . .'

It all took time, and the pile of correspondence mounted in
Joe's office with the arrival of another mail delivery. But it
was worth it. Each visit transformed a remote relationship
into a friendly personal acquaintance and who could tell into
what fresh areas of human need it would lead?

But the pile of correspondence had to be dealt with, and
Joe sometimes said he couldn't get down to work until the
offices were closed, and he was free of interruptions. But even
then, he could not be sure of a clear period. On one occasion,
long after dark, an unexpected visitor arrived providing him
with an opportunity never likely to be repeated.

It was a rainy, blustery winter evening, about four hours
after everyone else had left when, sitting at his desk, he heard
the front door bell ring down below. He thought at first it
might be some children playing around, but then he realised it
was not the sort of weather in which anyone would be out
without a reason, and that door bell was still being rung. So
he ran down the stairs, across the showroom, and unlocking
the front door was somewhat taken aback when the slight
figure of a woman, shrouded in a mackintosh, slipped past
him into the room.

'I want some New Testaments in Arabic,' she said, and then
told him she had arrived in London by private plane that day,
to escort a very important person to hospital. His eyes opened
wide when she mentioned the name of the Middle East
country from which she had come. 'And I'm going back by
private plane tomorrow,' she went on. She did not tell him
much more, but the mention of that country, and the fact that
she had come by private plane was sufficient. She evidently
had entry into a circle where some of the wealthiest Arabs in
the world moved, and somewhere among them were

individuals wanting to read the New Testament in their own language. 'I'm so thankful someone was here,' she said. 'This is the only chance I have to get those New Testaments. There are people who want them...'

Joe nodded, pointed to a chair for her to sit down, and off he went into the warehouse, found six New Testaments in Arabic, and gave them to her. She thanked him, pressed £40 into his hand, disappeared into the night, and he heard from her no more. He did not even know her name. But a year later he received a letter from a young teacher in North America, saying, 'I've just returned from a stint of teaching in...' Joe read, and his interest quickened as he read the name of the country. 'Do you remember giving some New Testaments in Arabic to a woman who came to your office one night? I just want you to know that wonderful things happened as a result of those New Testaments...' No details were given, but the young writer urged, 'Keep up the good work!'

9

The Production Manager

Like every other human organisation SGM, at its core, is a
body of men and women on whose work and initiative it
depends for its effectiveness. However up to date its
machinery, however ample its supply of money, without the
right people to use both, it is slowed down, and could even be
brought to a halt. Obtaining the right people for the right jobs
has always been one of its major objectives. Faith, prayer and
patience have been exercised as much for obtaining staff as
for obtaining money. With its policy of only employing as
members of staff those who are committed Christians, it has
precluded some who would otherwise have done the work
required efficiently enough, but would have failed to bring
the necessary ingredient of spiritual life. On the other hand,
its standards of production have demanded that its workers
should be skilful in their particular spheres.

But there has been something else. Mighell Smith
summarised the Mission's ideal when he said, 'We want
people who are called by God into this work.' God had called
and equipped Bezalel for his practical work in the tabernacle
in the wilderness, and there was no reason to believe He did
not call and equip people in the same way, and for the same
practical purposes, in the twentieth century. The conviction
of that calling had kept Mighell Smith himself in SGM for
over thirty years, and the same could be said, he knew, of the
men and women who had served alongside him through the

years since the explosion and fire that had threatened to bring
it all to an end. In the event, the very disaster had been a
means of bringing unsought publicity which had resulted in
wider interest and support. The widening interest had been of
special value in the years of change that had followed it.

It was in 1960 that Harold Macmillan made his famous
'wind of change' speech, and change had certainly character-
ised the decade of 'the swinging sixties', nationally and
internationally. In the United Kingdom legislation that lifted
the ban on certain social habits had ushered in the permissive
society, while internationally, with country after country
gaining independence, colonialism was rapidly coming to an
end. New nations raised their flags, changed their names, and
declared themselves to be republics. New governments
introduced new regulations, and missionaries in lands where
they had been free to live and work, now found themselves
restricted, and in some cases even forced to leave. In many
places civil war had broken out, resulting in the movement of
whole communities as members of races that had been settled
in lands for centuries started scattering all over the world.
Refugees and immigrants had flowed into the United
Kingdom to create a multi-racial society, and the same thing
had happened in other countries of the affluent West.

The political scene was like a kaleidoscope that had been
touched by an invisible hand, changing the pattern entirely as
the same little discs reappeared in a completely different
setting.

All this had had its effect on SGM. Internationally, it had
become increasingly evident that the production in new
languages and the distribution of the Scripture booklets
would depend less on expatriates and more on national
Christians. The decision of the Council to make overseas
distribution a priority and to send senior staff members
abroad to see for themselves where the needs and
opportunities lay had been made at the right time. New
personal relationships were formed with Christian leaders in

countries in Asia and Africa, as well as in Europe, and in 1965
Mighell Smith reported that some 20,000 distributors were in
direct touch with members of headquarters staff. While in
1972, writing his annual letter to supporters, he said, 'It is a
great, perhaps unique privilege to be in touch with Christian
workers in almost every country in the world.' On them, to a
great extent, depended the extension of the work, the
accuracy of translations, and the effective distribution of the
booklets, though he did not mention it. He merely pointed
out that this wide range of contacts gave SGM an insight into
how the Holy Spirit was working in the world of today,
revealing His power in the contemporary scene, and
continued, 'It leads us to see the need for redoubled efforts to
discern the will of God in all our production plans.'

Our production plans.

Production covered a wide range of aspects, not least the
very mundane matter of ensuring that SGM publications
were on good quality paper, and that the art work was both
attractive and appropriate. Appearances were important –
not as an end in themselves, but in order to influence the
customer, as the businessman would put it, in favour of the
commodity. In this case the commodity was the Word of
God, and must be presented in a way that would appeal, not
deter. Countless numbers of people had read the words
contained in an SGM leaflet because in the first place they
simply liked the look of it. The standard had to be
maintained, and at a time when heavy inflation was
increasing costs to an alarming extent, and when the
Mission's income was not rising fast enough to keep pace
with it, the job of the Production Manager was one that no
one envied. Furthermore, its scope had increased over the
years with the wider production and distribution of its
publications in other countries. The choice of illustrations,
paper, and general production to suit the varying cultures of
animistic tribes and sophisticated urban dwellers in many
countries was his responsibility, in addition to the more

obvious task of obtaining the best paper and the most reliable printers at the lowest price.

When Mighell Smith made reference to discerning the will of God in the Mission's production plans, he may well have had in mind a problem that was beginning to loom up for the Council. Over the horizon of the future was the fact that the Production Manager, who had filled the position for nearly thirty years, who understood the department through and through, was coming up for retirement, and no one was in view to take his place.

Someone with a professional knowledge of printing, with business acumen, and if possible with experience in other countries besides Great Britain was required, and where was he to be found? Other departments had had their needs met, as, for example, when a missionary from Zambia joined the translation team, and a young woman from Switzerland arrived at a time when the work in French-speaking Europe needed reinforcing. All the same, there was no denying the fact that there had been serious delays in production and output through shortage of staff, and at this stage the lack of the right man for the job that required a combination of several abilities could prove almost crippling. But at the beginning of 1972, the year that proved to be the very last of the Production Manager's life, it began to emerge that God had been preparing the right man to fill his place.

The inner story of the Mission is rather like a tapestry in which many living threads are brought together by a Master hand, appearing, then sometimes disappearing for a time, to reappear as the pattern develops. In some cases those living threads are introduced very early, and Roger Kennedy is a case in point.

At the age of eleven Roger Kennedy was a 'Lone Searcher'. How ardently he searched, history does not relate, but as his parents were enthusiastic supporters of SGM and frequently entertained deputation speakers in their home, he was given an insight into its character at an early age. It was those deputation speakers who made a deep impression on the schoolboy, for like his own father, they were family men, and took an interest in children. One of them was to play a vitally important part in his future life although, of course, he had no idea of it at the time.

When Norman Brown came to his home representing SGM, Roger Kennedy recognised him as one of the officers he had met at a youth camp in Cumbria. Norman Brown had been in shorts then, but now he was neatly and suitably clad, ready to ascend the platform and address a meeting. But he was as interesting and inspiring a speaker off the platform as on it, and always had a fund of stories to relate over the tea-table:

A British minesweeper, converted into a missionary ship by Finnish Christians, dropped anchor in the Pool of London to take on board supplies of Bibles, New Testaments, and other SGM material, enroute for India to cruise up and down its rivers, that the Word of God might be proclaimed and distributed...

A young man who had worked in the SGM warehouse for a time, then went to the Middle East as a missionary and before he could even speak the language started preaching by proxy, as he visited lonely bays to give SGM leaflets to Arab fishermen, walked along narrow alleys to hand out, here and there, leaflets to Arab tradesmen...

A hospital visitor who always went armed with SGM leaflets and reported 'One man kept a copy in his pyjama pocket and read it constantly. It led him into a real knowledge of Christ, and he died a bright Christian...

Nor were Norman Brown's stories only about people who had been spiritually awakened through reading 'the little books' as he called them. One of his favourite topics was about the people who he asserted were the backbone of the work. For the most part they were poor people, unknown, unimportant by the world's standards, but as he saw it, the Mission would soon peter out if such people ceased to support it.

There was the old couple, Fred and Martha, for instance, who lived frugally in a small cottage. They kept it beautifully clean and tidy, but obviously had little enough money to spend on it. Norman Brown knew them well, was touched by the donations for SGM received regularly, and always saw to it that those donations received a special personal letter of thanks. Then Fred died, and Martha was left alone.

One day, when SGM funds were rather low, a little packet arrived from Martha. It contained two golden sovereigns, memorials of two of the most significant events in Fred's life. One was his first week's wages, the other was his wedding gift to Martha.

Norman Brown tried to picture her as she picked up those two coins, looked at them, perhaps with tears in her eyes, then deliberately packed them up and sent them off. It was not difficult to know the reaction of the One to whom she had given those two coins. The story had been told to countless multitudes down through the centuries, of a time when Jesus was in the temple at Jerusalem, watching the rich men coming and casting their gifts into the treasury, and what He said of the two mites a poor widow threw into the same treasure chest. 'She has thrown in more than any of them! She has given all that she had!' And since that same Lord had revealed His power to make five loaves and two fishes enough to feed 5,000 people, it was not difficult to believe He would do as much, and more, with those two gold sovereigns.

Then there were the two old sisters, aged ninety and ninety-two, whom he went to visit when he was on deputation in Wales, near their home. 'In my comparatively youthful enthusiasm I thought I could bring them some cheer,' he laughed and soon discovered that they were in no need of enlivenment. They chatted with animation about things in general and SGM in particular, and then the younger of them said something he never forgot.

'For over sixty years I have been praying for the work of SGM – praying every day.'

For sixty years! Praying for the Mission since before he was born! He got a glimpse that day of the invisible reason for the Mission's continuity.

'I think it is typical of so many elderly friends of ours,' he said when he related the incident. 'And that, I am sure, is the real strength of the work.'

Even more personal was the story of May, who lived in Cornwall. She had no legs, was crippled with rheumatoid arthritis, but was perfectly content for, as she said when he visited her, 'The Lord Jesus is here, and I speak to Him and He speaks to me, so what more do I want?' Then she carefully opened a little bundle of paper, tied together with wool, and extracted the current Prayer Fellowship, leaflet. 'Look there,' she said, and he was touched to see written there his own name, and that of his secretary, and to hear her say, 'I pray for you every day.'

Such stories, were almost as frequent and even more moving, than those of conversions of people in far off countries. Altogether, Roger Kennedy's heart warmed towards the Mission, and one day, in his teens, he wrote to Mr Brown explaining that he was interested in Christian literature work, and wondered if there would be a job for him in SGM when he left school.

Headquarters staff at SGM were not unaccustomed to receiving applications from quite unsuitable people. Well-meaning Christian workers, in particular, had a habit of getting in touch with the enquiry, 'I wonder if you can find a job for someone I know – just become a Christian – no, no particular qualifications, but would be willing to learn, I'm sure – to be in a place like yours would be such a help...'

The reply to such requests was invariably polite, but also

firm. SGM had a very high standard of work which must be maintained, so those employed must not only be Christians but also have the necessary qualifications and experience for their jobs.

In the case of Roger, the answer was simple for the Mission rarely took anyone who had not had commercial experience. 'Get your training, prove yourself in a secular job, and come back!'

Twenty years later, having done just that, he came back.

In the intervening twenty years he had taken printing training, gone to India to help establish the Christian publishing house, Masihi Sahitya Sanstha in Delhi, travelled in countries of the Far East, training nationals in the techniques of literature production and distribution, and in the midst of these varied activities he had always managed to maintain contact with SGM.

And Norman Brown had maintained contact with him, following his career perhaps more closely than Roger realised. He knew what he had been doing, knew that he and his wife had agreed his task was not only to see the publishing house established, but Indians in control. And he knew when the end of their service in India was due. So one day he asked them directly, 'What are you going to do when you come home? Our Production Manager, who has been in that position for nearly thirty years, is coming up for retirement, and there is no one to take his place.'

No one could have foreseen that, with the sudden death of the Production Manager, the position would fall vacant even earlier than had been anticipated. But by that time the Kennedys had just returned from India, and the 'Lone Searcher' of thirty years ago was ready to step into the gap.

The man who had written to him then, telling him to get his training, prove himself in a secular job, and then come back, was ready to step into a gap, too. Mighell Smith was due for retirement, Norman Brown was appointed into his position as Secretary, and found himself at the helm.

10

Needed – The Men for the Job

Being at the helm of SGM entailed a great deal more than
sitting in an office at headquarters and overseeing the work
from there, as Norman Brown very well knew. In fact, there
were times when he was away for weeks on end, on
deputation work in the UK and occasionally for months
visiting the overseas branches.

When he joined the staff in 1944 he had not envisaged
world travel as being part of his duty. Not that it would have
deterred him. Indeed, he might even have found it more to his
taste then than when he embarked on those journeys thirty
years later. But by the time he became leader of the work he
knew the value and importance of maintaining personal
relationships with the workers in the SGM offices in
Zimbabwe and South Africa, Canada and the USA,
Australia and New Zealand, and India. Although, including
Scotland and Ireland, they were distributed over all five
continents, he made it his business to visit them all.

Those visits brought to life some of the people who
otherwise might merely have been names on a list, like Joel in
the branch in Zimbabwe (formerly Southern Rhodesia).

The branch in Zimbabwe was the one most recently
opened, three years after the fire. It had been started by an
enterprising businessman who was a Council member, and
who had recently helped to launch SGM in South Africa.
Like Frank Henman, who was Chairman of the Council for

Needed – The Men for the Job   109

so many years, he was a man with vision. Having seen the
Mission established in South Africa, he realised there was a
need and an opportunity to do the same in Zimbabwe. So in
1959 a suite in an office block on one of the main streets in the
capital was rented by Scripture Gift Mission. It was stocked
with booklets and leaflets, not only in English, not only in the
two main tribal languages of the country, but in seven or eight
other languages as well. A staff of three or four was engaged,
comprising both European and African workers. Samples of
what the Mission could supply were sent out to churches and
mission stations throughout the country, irrespective of
denomination. The literature contained only extracts from
the Bible, so was equally acceptable to all. And through them
the information was filtered that portions of God's Word
were available in Ndau, Ndebele, Nambya, Nyania, Shona,
Tonga, Tswana, Tsonga, Nsenga, Venda – and that they
would be given away free of charge to those who came to get
them, and promised to read or distribute them wisely.

The news got round, and things started to move. In ones or
twos, or little groups, Africans started coming in from the
bush, along the wide, tree-lined streets of the capital, looking
for the office block with the right number. Rather diffidently
they entered the foyer, walked across to the lift, pressed the
button, and were conveyed to the first floor. There they saw
the words Scripture Gift Mission, and knew they had come to
the right place. In the reception room they saw two desks and
a few chairs, and a smiling European who invited them to sit
down.

The difficulty started when she spoke to them in English,
and they couldn't understand what she said. Or, if they
understood and replied as best they could, she couldn't
understand them. It might have been awkward, but the
difficulty was solved as soon as she disappeared through a
door and returned in half a minute saying, 'This is Joel. He
will help you.' And they saw behind her a fellow-African
beaming at them, and addressing them, not in English, but in

Shona. Yes he understood them. It did not matter to which
tribe they belonged, Joel could nearly always communicate.
Let them come through to the stock room, and he would find
for them just the booklets they wanted, in their own language.
And some time later the European receptionist would see
them emerge, brimming over with gratitude and glowing with
joy as they held in their hands for the first time a portion of
God's word that they could read and understand, and that
was their own personal possession. And when they had left,
the European receptionist and Joel would look at each other,
and they would glow, too. The visits of those Africans from
their little villages of thatched huts in the bush were highlights
in their days, and they shared their sense of satisfaction in
that understanding glance before she returned to her
accounts and he to his packing.

For Joel was the packer. That was his job. Day after day he
made up bundles and packages of literature to fulfil the
requests that came in from all over the country, and even
beyond. So many of the Africans were only semi-literate, and
the booklets which condensed the Gospel in words of
Scripture that they could understand were in great demand.
Joel was kept busy from morning to night. But he was more
than a packer. To hear his rich full voice uplifted in prayer, to
see him counselling in their own languages the visitors who
came into the office, was to see a pastor in his element, and
Norman Brown wrote warmly of him in his report.

'Joel, aged fifty, has been with us for thirteen years. Within
his own church he is entitled to be called a Bishop, but he
doesn't take the title. He was the one who was approached to
be a sub-chief, but declined because it would involve him in
the old ritual practices which he felt were not for a Christian.

'Joel is quite a linguist. His national language is Shona,
which is the language of the majority of Africans in this area,
but he knows two or three others, and therefore is useful in
translating some of the letters that come into the office.'
Without Joel, who could tell how many orders would have
been delayed, or gone astray?

There was something else about Joel that Norman Brown did not fail to notice. It was his smart appearance. 'Joel and his assistant both wear collars and ties and waistcoats, even when they are packing,' he observed, adding that he wondered how they managed when the weather was really hot. He thought the packers back there in London would be interested in the little sidelight on their African counterpart.

He had the opportunity to see Joel in another capacity, too, when he went to one of the African townships to speak by interpretation at a meeting, at which massed choirs provided inspiring musical items. 'Joel brought his family along to sing, one piece in Shona, one in English. As he has eleven children, and only one, the eldest, was not present, he was able to provide a choir from his own home.'

Altogether, it would be difficult to assess how much of the work's success, with conversions reported even from among the terrorists as a result of reading SGM booklets, was due to the steady, faithful service of a packer in the branch in Zimbabwe.

Over in Canada, he met another staff member on whose steady background work so much had depended. She was one, however, to whom he needed no introduction. Lenore Wilkinson came from Cheshire where, as a schoolgirl, she had joined the Young Searchers' League, and had received Christ into her life. Norman Brown, then in charge of the SGM office in Liverpool, met her some time later, and invited her to join the staff. She remained on the staff even when she moved to Canada, for SGM had an office in Toronto, and she was there when news of the fire and the destruction of the familiar old headquarters in London came as a devastating blow, especially as the former Secretary had retired, and she was more or less in charge. 'But we all proved the wonderful provision of our God,' and the little branch weathered the storm though it was seriously affected by the losses incurred. Furthermore, its outreach was effective and widespread. One who later became a Council member was first drawn to SGM when he saw the use made of its leaflets and booklets by missionaries to the shanty men in the backwoods. Then, as President of the Andes Evangelical Mission, he was stirred by what he heard of its effectiveness in a remote village in South America. Some villagers, high in the Andes mountains, had expressed a desire to know the Gospel, but there was no one to go to them. However, one of the Mission's pilots flew over their village from time to time, swooping low and dropping SGM leaflets and booklets in their language. Eventually a Bolivian evangelist and a missionary visited them, and to their utter surprise, after preaching to the villagers for the first time, the headman stood up and said, 'I am ready.'

'Ready for what?'

'Ready to become a Christian.' Eight others made the same affirmation, and all gave a clear expression of faith in Jesus Christ as Saviour and Lord. The two preachers enquired how, after only hearing the Gospel once, they had so complete an understanding of it. It was mystifying!

'But we have been reading the little books you dropped from your plane,' the villagers replied, simply. That was how they knew what it meant to be a Christian, and that is why some of them were prepared to act on what they now believed. They saw nothing surprising in that. The little books contained words that God had spoken and their hearts had responded to what they read, and now they were ready...

From such diverse places as the backwoods of northern Canada and the Andes in South America came evidence of the effect of the Word of God, and the Council member in Toronto wrote feelingly, 'How we bless God for those who pioneer, who translate, who give their lives to supply the Scriptures in a form to be read and understood!'

As Norman Brown travelled to the various branches, he heard many such stories to stimulate his enthusiasm for his job. Although his visits were mainly concerned with what are termed the mechanics of the work, business methods, finance, distribution, production, and especially the maintaining of cordial, understanding relationships, the purpose of it all was to bring life to people who were spiritually dead. And in every branch to which he went there were such stories, not only of dramatic conversions, but of strengthening and comfort brought in times of special strain. There was the hospital chaplain in New Zealand who reported, 'During the years of my ministry on both parish and hospital chaplaincy, I made frequent and blessed use of SGM booklets.

'Many a patient on being readmitted for treatment has brought with him or her a copy of *Daily Strength* given long ago. I have also seen patients being wheeled for surgery with their copy of the same firmly clutched in their hand. They simply would not leave the known for the unknown without the comfort and strength of the Word of God.' When he himself was found to have cancer and retired from his chaplaincy, he continued his visitation to cancer patients in their own homes, always 'armed for the conflict' as he put it, with copies of *Daily Strength.* 'I advise them to familiarise themselves with the texts, and so draw near to the God of all comfort, and shut out the negative thoughts that so easily come to folk with cancer.' As one of themselves now, he could speak with the greater conviction. As he was also a regular broadcaster on the national radio, his influence was wide, and his correspondence heavy. His requests for further copies of *Daily Strength* were usually for 500 at a time.

One of the difficulties Norman Brown constantly encountered as he visited the branches was the same as he encountered at home – the difficulty of obtaining the right staff. 'In each branch I visited last year, as here in London, there are urgent staff needs,' he wrote at the end of one of his overseas tours. The need for someone to head up the work in Australia had been evident for some time, and when he wrote that sentence the need was still there. What neither he nor anyone else could have known at the time was that as far back as 1968 a man was being prepared for the position.

It was the year in which Joe Carroll went to India to help in the branch in Bangalore, and one of the grants he made at that time was to a young missionary named Geoff Richards, who asked for a supply of Christmas leaflets. He wanted them for distribution in a smuggling village north of Bombay, where he had the opportunity to preach on the true meaning of Christmas. He had been conducting a small weekly Bible study with a group of young people there, some of whom did not hesitate to try and sell him 'at a very good discount' Japanese sewing machines that had been smuggled in. After all, smuggling was their job! But it was through the persuasion of one of these young people that the local Roman Catholic priest had been prevailed upon to invite him to preach in his church, and Geoff Richards wisely decided he would base his sermon solely on the Word of God. That is why he applied to Joe for the Christmas leaflets, which he distributed among the 200 people (including four Roman Catholic priests) who gathered for the meeting. Then he simply enlarged on the texts in the leaflets. 'This is what the Bible says,' and no one could argue against it.

That very evening the leader of the young people's group, sitting quietly in the church, reading and listening to the texts, put his faith in Christ.

It was the beginning of a movement that spread over a wide area. The youth leader was followed by a number of others who believed and were baptised, until some years later there was a strong Christian community in the neighbourhood. Geoff Richards always traced the commencement of that work to the simple reading and expounding of God's Word in those little SGM booklets at a Christmas service in a Roman Catholic church. It was the first time he had used them in that way, and he never forgot it. In India, and later in the Middle East, he constantly applied to the Mission for their booklets in a variety of languages because he observed that where they were introduced conviction, repentance and faith seemed to follow. The experience of those years provided an incentive to accept eventually the position of Federal Secretary in what was to prove the much harder field of Australia.

By and large, things went smoothly for SGM in the 1970s, although for a long period, paper shortages and rising prices put a strain on production. However, the work overseas was expanding, and as Norman Brown reviewed the year in his annual letter for 1979, he reported, 'We print in some thirty countries... with a greater output than ever.' And the contacts worldwide continued. 'More than in any previous year the Mission's staff has travelled. Ronald Young to the Far East, Roger Kennedy to India, which has a greater population than South America and Africa combined, Joe Carroll to Sri Lanka, and my own long overseas visits to the branches...' He had observed over it all the increasing disparity between wealth and poverty, the rapid closing of countries to Christianity, and the challenging fact that at least 3,000 languages and major dialects were still without any portion of Scripture.

It was about this time that one of the files that had been closed in the Translation Department was reopened. A letter had been received from Operation Mobilisation's head-quarters in Belgium, drawing attention to Afghanistan. It was one of the most neglected countries in the world, the writer pointed out, with only a handful of national believers among fifteen million fanatical Muslims and 'I strongly feel that now is the time we must move to take the Gospel to as many Afghans as possible.' As things were, there were many opportunities to distribute literature, to hand out Scripture portions in villages, but if present political trends continued the doors might be shut within a few years. SGM was therefore urged to undertake the printing of *God's Plan for Man* and *The Glory of Christ* as quickly as possible in a language that was spoken and understood by five million people. Two or three suggestions were made regarding possible help with the necessary translation.

So the file on the Afghan language, Dari, was reopened. To the stream of correspondence that went out from Ken Andrewartha's department were added questionnaires, queries, letters all relating to the translation of the two leaflets into Dari.

It was only one of a number of new translations for people who had nothing – the Tuaregs of the Sahara, the Kanyok of Zaire, and others. But there was an urgency about this one. The political scene was darkening in Afghanistan, and it seemed that in the race against time anything in the Dari language might be produced too late. Furthermore, it was numerically important. The Tuaregs could be numbered in hundreds, there were an estimated 150,000 Kanyoks, but the Afghans numbered five million.

Winifred Marden, whose job it was to be aware of what was going on in the world, noted very carefully any reference to the news of Communist advances in Afghanistan.

So the new decade began, and for SGM the 1980s started with financial testing. The first few months were normal enough, but by the time September came it was evident to the Secretary and the Council that if things continued as they had been going for some weeks, the Mission would run into debt. So for the first time that any of the new members of staff could remember, it was decided that production must be curtailed, and additional time be given to prayer.

For the junior members of staff it was a solemnising experience. One young secretary who had only recently joined the staff was challenged and rather inspired to hear the older, mature leaders of the work praying fervently for the financial provision without which the Mission must cease to exist. The prayer meetings were times of heart-searching and confession – had we taken our provision for granted, failed to give God the glory? There was affirmation of faith, as some of the well-tried promises like, 'seek first his kingdom and his righteousness, and all these things will be given to you as well' were reiterated with confidence. Winifred almost held her breath as her own faith swung between doubt and assurance during those days of uncertainty. And how could she express the thrill of relief, amounting to exultation, as announcements began to be made of large gifts arriving almost out of the blue, of an increased flow of smaller ones, of the rising of the balance at the bank, of orders for urgently needed printing being put in hand again, and eventually of thankfulness to God that the immediate crisis was over, and finances were on an even keel once more. That young secretary's confidence in the Mission was even stronger after that experience than it had been before – and in the God upon whom the organisation so evidently relied.

In 1982 another crisis occurred. This time it was one that altered the whole nation, and had no direct bearing on SGM. Argentinian Forces landed on the Falkland Islands, the Prime Minister ordered a British Task Force to proceed immediately to the South Pacific, and for weeks the conflict there was headline news. The chief effect it had on SGM was to bring into focus one of its departments, which became the centre of accelerated activity, with a sudden increase of telephone calls, comings and goings, hurried consultations and priority orders to the Production and Packing Departments.

In some ways, the department in question was quite different from the others, for it was older than any of them, older even than the SGM itself. To trace it to its source, we must turn back the pages of history two hundred years...

11

Serving the Services

Nationally and internationally things were rather tense for Great Britain in the year 1780. What with the Spanish besieging Gibraltar, the Americans fighting for independence, and threats of trouble in the West Indies, her Armed Forces were being kept busy. On top of that, there were so many riots in London that the Army had been called in. It no doubt helped to subdue the unruly elements in society, but at the same time created problems of its own. Some battalions were stationed in Hyde Park, and although the men in their scarlet uniforms were smart and well disciplined enough on parade, they were for ever getting involved in drunken brawls and generally making a nuisance of themselves when off duty. The floggings and detention in chains they brought on themselves as punishment did little to deter them. They had nothing to do but roam the streets, terrorising in peace the very people they would be defending in war, and with nowhere to go but to the inns and gin-palaces.

It was the sight of these uniformed men in the heart of the capital that stirred a Christian man to action. Something must be done for their spiritual welfare, and he decided to call a public meeting to consider the matter. His idea was to form a society to supply them with Bibles, and anticipating a ready response from the church-going public to his advertising he booked a large hall in the vicinity of Fleet Street for the occasion. He arrived in good time and waited expectantly, but no one turned up. Eventually, sitting down on the platform he was gathering together his papers when he heard the sound of footsteps mounting the stairs. The door opened, and in walked a well-dressed, dignified man whom he had never seen before. The stranger glanced round in surprise, and said, 'I've come here in answer to an advertisement announcing a meeting for a purpose of which I highly approve. Have I mistaken the time?'

'No, you have not mistaken the time,' he was told by the somewhat dejected convenor. 'I called the meeting for this hour, but you are the only person who has come. I suppose we had better go home.'

But the stranger would have none of it. Go home, having accomplished nothing? Certainly not! 'I approve of your plan and believe it will succeed.' He was all for getting down to business, then and there.

'But what can we do?'

'What can we do? We can propose, second and carry resolutions!'

The Chairman sat up. The suggestion was daring, yet ludicrous. Certainly there was nothing to prevent them from proposing, seconding and carrying resolutions, but . . .

'But what can we say about this meeting?' he asked.

'Say?' retorted the energetic stranger. 'We can say that we proposed, seconded and carried unanimously resolutions at a publicly convened meeting of which due notice had been given to the press.

'It is true we cannot say it was well attended,' he conceded, 'but we can assert that it was respectably attended, and that's more than can be said about some public meetings! Come, sir, propose the resolutions and I will second them.' So various suitable resolutions were duly proposed, seconded and carried unanimously, and the meeting was adjourned. Another meeting was later convened, and with greater numbers attending, including some well-known philanthropists. The society was given the simple name The Bible

Society, and by the end of July that year the distribution of Bibles to soldiers had started.

In spite of its inauspicious birth, by the year 1822 it had grown into a healthy and highly respected organisation, with His Royal Highness the Duke of York as its patron, His Grace the Archbishop of Canterbury as its president, and no less than forty-one vice-presidents, all of whom, with one exception, were dukes and earls, admirals or major-generals, baronets or bishops, or at the very least, deans. The only exception in this illustrious list of titled dignitaries, the only one who could claim no other title than a mere esquire, was William Wilberforce.

When the British and Foreign Bible Society was formed in the year 1804 The Bible Society changed its name to Naval and Military Bible Society to define more clearly its sphere of service. It could change its name, but nothing could change its history or its claim to being the first known Bible Society of its kind in the British Isles. It continued as an independent organisation until early in the twentieth century when, at the instigation of Bishop Taylor Smith, the Chaplain General, and at the request of the Charity Commissioners, it was brought into association with Scripture Gift Mission.

This took place in 1910. Four years later the First World War broke out, and the value of the union of the two organisations became evident. The financial resources and expertise of Scripture Gift Mission, allied to the name of the Naval and Military Bible Society, provided just the instrument by which millions of copies of the Scriptures were distributed to the men in the Forces. The crowning inspiration of the pocket-sized New Testaments that were specially produced for the men of the Fleet was the crest of the Royal Navy embossed on each cover.

The crest of the Royal Navy! The crest of the very Force in which they served! The men were obviously gratified. Somehow that crest made the gift of the little book more significant and personal. The idea was so successful in the

Navy that before long New Testaments were being produced
with an Army crest and later, when the Air Force was added
to the Naval and Military Bible Society, with that crest, too.

The "crested" Scriptures, as they were called, were widely
distributed to the chaplains who could use them, and in the
1980s they are in as great a demand as when they made their
first appearance, whether Bibles, New Testaments or
Gospels.

It has to be admitted that the crest meant more to many of
the recipients than the contents. The SGM committee
responsible for putting in fresh orders often spent hours
discussing the relative merits of the Revised Standard
Version, the Good News version, the New International
Version, all of which SGM were now using. Most were
agreed that very few young people could understand the
language of the Authorised Version, but with at least three
modern versions to choose from, which should it be for the
men and women in the Forces? (For the record, "crested"
Scriptures are now produced in all three.) But as one chaplain
observed drily, 'I find in the Army Cadet Force... that it is
the crest on the Gospel which appeals, whichever the version
used!'

It was the crest that caught the eye, providing the initial
motive for possession. William Walters' contention that
appearances matter was constantly being justified. The little
book might be tucked away in a pocket or even at the bottom
of a trunk for days, months, years, but who could tell when in
a lonely outpost, or in a time of danger, or even boredom, it
would be extracted and opened and read? At that point the
importance of the version chosen became evident.

'It was a stroke of genius to produce a New Testament in
language that the average soldier could understand, and in a
size and cover that make it virtually indestructible, even in a
combat situation,' wrote one chaplain appreciatively. And
who could tell the effect that reading those divinely inspired
words would have? One young man doing National Service

in the 1950s received one, and three decades later in 1986 wrote:

> No doubt you get many letters of appreciation. My own appreciation dates from 1950 when, as a raw recruit to the RAF as a National Serviceman I was given my first Bible by the NM & AFBS.* That gift was part of my own conversion, and I trust the Gospels I issue on your behalf will help to convert others.

He was a chaplain in the Air Training Corps who had written for a supply of Gospels with ATC crests on them. 'They will be of great help in the ministry to the cadets of my squadron.'

But the crest had another function, as one RAF chaplain pointed out, urging the importance of continuing their production.

'We feel that this is a practice which should continue. If the practice ceases, it might well be construed that our Service commitment is incompatible with the material contained in the Holy Scriptures.' As long as the Chaplain's Department, with its duty to uphold Christian doctrines and ethics was an integral part of the Ministry of Defence, the crests on the Bibles would be appropriate.

The link that the Secretary of the Society had with the Chaplain's Department was productive in other ways, too. In 1968 the Army introduced into its curriculum a Character Training Scheme for young cadets, with an emphasis on integrity and self-control. SGM produced a series of leaflets to go along with it. Intriguing titles like *Voices In My Mind*, *Food For Thought* and *The Voice of Conscience* appearing on the bookstall attracted the attention of young cadets moving out of church after services, and keen-eyed chaplains noticed those who took them. They would provide a useful talking point later on. The chaplains put them to other uses, too. As one wrote:

---

*The name of the society is Naval Military and Air Force Bible Society.

For ten years I took regular Sunday services. The booklets were a source of interest and I used them as a basis for my short addresses. Never once did I miss saying that they were for placing on their side tables for reading at night, and for keeping in their Bibles ... many of the chaps did read them, and numbers asked for spare copies.

The crested Bibles and the production of booklets and leaflets suitable for young men had proved invaluable to chaplains in the Armed Forces of Great Britain for many years by the time Eric Cook went to West Africa, and saw the inauguration of the same scheme in Ghana. Twenty years later Bibles with the crest of the Ghanaian Armed Forces were still in demand.

When the Falklands crisis flared up, therefore, it was natural that chaplains already in touch with the NM & AFBS should turn to it for the extra supplies of Scriptures they would need in the emergency. Almost before it was known that a Task Force would be proceeding to the faraway islands the chaplain of HMS Hermes had written to say he would appreciate a supply of Bibles and New Testaments.

Bernard Dodd, Travelling Secretary to the Society, saw to it that they were sent off immediately. Prior to the sailing of the liner Queen Elizabeth II he went personally to deliver the parcels of Scriptures that were to go on board. He found it very moving to go to the homes of the chaplains who would be using them, the chaplains who were preparing to go with the men of the Armed Forces down to the South Atlantic. He remembered vividly his own feelings when, as a young serviceman, he had been in Germany during the Berlin air lift. The city was surrounded by Russian troops, leaving the British and American soldiers in it marooned as on a tiny island in the midst of an angry sea that threatened to submerge them. The tension of those days, living under the menacing possibility of war breaking out, was brought back to him as he went into the homes of those chaplains. Very soon they would be boarding the ship that was to take them, along with the hundreds of young soldiers who were their spiritual responsibility, to face an unknown enemy on an unknown territory, thousands of miles away from any friendly shore.

'A number of nominal Christians have entered into a new spiritual experience, and others into a deeper commitment', was the encouraging news that came back to him later, but with it was a request that struck a solemn note. It was for booklets for bereaved relatives. The war had claimed its victims.

Months later he met those chaplains again, shortly after their return. They had already been to visit young widows and grieving parents, and he saw the toll it had taken of them emotionally. His contacts with chaplains in the Armed Forces brought home to him again and again the uneasiness of a world where peace is poised on a very insecure edge, and a letter of thanks from one of them for Bibles that had been supplied impressed him further:

> I am chaplain to a TA Signal Regiment whose role is to provide Home Defence communications for the civil authorities in the event of a nuclear war. Part of their mobilisation will involve waiting in a scattered number of locations until they are needed to provide communications. I have distributed the Bibles throughout the Regiment so that each troop or squadron has one for its use.

To be living with the constant reminder of the possibility of nuclear warfare could impose an unconscious strain on the nerves, and Bernard Dodd was glad of his own experience during the days of the Berlin air lift. He could feel for young men in situations of sustained tension, like those who were billeted in Northern Ireland. But he had another reason for being glad of those days in Germany. It was at that very time, living under the threat of imprisonment or death at the hand of an enemy, that he turned to Christ as Saviour. Nor was he alone in doing so. Through the convincing testimony of one man, some thirty others besides himself had put their faith in the One who has promised everlasting happiness in the world that is to come. Safety and security rarely prove to be as good a preparation spiritually as do uncertainty and danger.

Perhaps that is why requests for grants of literature came so frequently from padres in Northern Ireland, and met with such a prompt and sympathetic response. Not that every request could always be fully met. 'We could have distributed many more if we had had the necessary funds to provide them,' Bernard Dodd reported sadly on more than one occasion. In 1981 there was a noticeable fall in distribution figures, and he had to explain to his Committee that the reason for it was not a fall in requests for the Scriptures, but the need to ration the supplies. 'If resources were available, the number of crested New Testaments granted would far surpass all former statistics.'

The Falklands crisis and the long drawn out tension in Northern Ireland focussed attention on the opportunities among the Armed Forces in those areas, but a letter from the senior chaplain to the British Forces on the Rhine, putting in a large order for New Testaments, contained a timely reminder that the major part of the British Army was stationed in Germany.

Although Bernard Dodd himself had become a Christian while an electrician in the RAF, he had had no thought then of doing the sort of work he was now engaged in. In fact, after leaving the Forces he trained for the Baptist ministry, and by 1973 was happily settled in Shepton Mallet, with neither desire nor expectation of leaving it, when a rather disturbing invitation reached him. It came from the chaplain of the Royal Naval Air Station at Yeovil, asking him to come and speak at a Christian fellowship family weekend, and to bring his wife and children with him.

Now Bernard Dodd was accustomed to his own pulpit, and

to addressing girls from the boarding school where the chaplain's own daughter was a pupil, but the idea of speaking to a group of naval men and their wives was strangely disconcerting, and he accepted the invitation with some trepidation. The weekend went well though, but he was not sorry when it was over, although it had prepared him for the suggestion contained in a letter he received a short time later. It was from the chaplain, explaining that the NM & AFBS would soon be needing a Travelling Secretary to take charge of the work, and asking if he would be willing to have his name put forward.

The suggestion was so unusual, so unexpected, that he felt he could not reject it out of hand. He knew perfectly well, from his study of the Bible, that God's call to Moses, to Gideon, to Jeremiah, to name but a few, had been equally unexpected. So he prayed about it, and thought about it, and eventually found himself being led to the conclusion that '*This is the way* – walk in it.' The outcome of it all was that less than a year later he was installed in a small office on the first floor of SGM, on the left of the corridor leading to the prayer room, and the recipient of a stream of letters and phone calls about Scriptures for the Armed Forces, and invitations to attend chaplains' conferences to introduce the work of his organisation. His predecessor Gowan Bishop, already a year overdue for retirement, spent two months initiating him into the work, travelling with him to, among other places, the Royal Naval College at Dartmouth, the Royal Air Force College at Cranwell, and a number of Army district headquarters to introduce him to the chaplains, and show him various key establishments. The object of the society he represented was summed up as follows:

The NM & AFBS is a missionary hearted enterprise. It believes that the circulation of the Word of God is the spearhead of evangelism. The Society's method of distributing the Holy Scriptures is to provide copies, without formal charge, to chaplains and other authorised workers with liberty to give or sell as circumstances indicate.

So he was launched into a new career in a constantly changing scene, with the closing of traditional service establishments such as the Chatham Naval Dockyard, the continuing run-down of British ports, and the introduction of women into Air Training Corps (ATC). As time passed, he had the opportunity of observing, through letters of thanks for Scriptures provided, which he received from chaplains, the changing trends among the young men in the services.

'During the year I seem to have taken a tremendous lot of rubbish from the ships' libraries, wrote one. 'A lot of seamen are reading horror or books on the occult. Five years ago it was sex, now it's horror.' On the other hand, there was an increasing interest in the Bible, which many of the young servicemen had never even handled before. The days when every child received an elementary knowledge of its contents when at school were past.

'The lads on board my submarine have never read a Bible in their lives before, and when the word got round that a supply of New Testaments had arrived, I was besieged with requests for copies...'

'I've been in Armagh with 3 Para for two months now and am beginning to feel, among some at least, an interest in the things of Christ. Some have asked for a copy of the Bible – many of the soldiers here have never opened a Bible's covers.'

'Another Good News Bible was passed on to a young airman this morning, as his first Bible, after his recent conversion.'

'I give the Bibles and New Testaments to prisoners in the guard rooms. Invariably they ask me rather than my having to offer them. Prisoners have time and solitude to read and reflect. And perhaps for remorse...'

'When preparing the New Testaments for presentation for

this Thursday's passing out parade, the Platoon Sergeant (a big, burly Jock!) asked if everyone got one. I said everyone got one on passing out. He said "I didn't – I've missed out, can I have one?" I offered him a full Good News Bible, which he declined. "I'd rather have the wee one I can carry about," he said.

'There's no doubt that most hold on to and treasure their New Testament,' the same writer continued. 'A few weeks ago, I was arranging the funeral service of a fifty-six-year-old officer, who had worked his way up from private to captain. His widow showed me his dog-eared little Testament which he still had amongst his treasures when he died. He'd kept it thirty-eight years. I've witnessed this dozens of times before.'

But Bernard Dodd soon discovered that his field of service was not confined to the Armed Forces. His predecessor had already made contact with a number of societies connected with the Merchant Navy. The Seaman's Christian Friends Society, Missions to Seamen, British Sailors' Society, Royal National Society to Deep Sea Fishermen, and a number of others were on the files, and through these organisations there was a wide opportunity for reaching, not only English speaking sailors, but those of other races.

The missioners who went aboard the merchant ships that berthed in their docks, sailing under a wide variety of flags, knew where to turn to for the leaflets in languages they themselves could not speak. 'You are often in my mind's eye, because as I go from ship to ship with abundant supplies, we are linked with you,' wrote one of them enthusiastically. 'I have been witnessing to the crew from a ship-wrecked vessel. Turks, Indians... great to give them your Scriptures. Thanks for all the supplies. We reach the world... spreading out on the ocean lanes to those far distant places.' Others wrote of passing on booklets and Gospels to sailors from such countries as Russia and mainland China, and from time to time a letter would arrive from a grateful recipient. One Polish merchant seaman wrote, 'I received your booklet, *The*

Tide is Turning, in Rotterdam. It was a really great event in my monotonous sea life. This booklet let me rouse my spirit. I am full of admiration for the writers and publishers. I would like to thank them for good time I got with this booklet. I would like to ask for New Testament.' There was no difficulty in obtaining one in his own language, and sending it to him.

Sitting there in the office on the first floor at SGM, it was encouraging to receive letters that indicated the arrival of parcels had come just at the right time.

'I have just come off a Samoan ship and have promised to return later. They are sailing at 20.30 hours. On reaching my base at the Crown Shipping Offices I found the two parcels you had sent, waiting for me. Imagine my joy on opening one of the parcels to find it contained Samoan literature. I can imagine their delight when I give them Scriptures in their own language. Thank you all!'

'Many thanks for the consignment which arrived safely this morning. That was quick work and very welcome, for we were desperate for Luke's Gospel for the children who come to our "Friday Special". We have been concentrating on this Gospel with them and there has been an excellent response from quite a number who have sought help on how to ask Jesus to be their Saviour.'

Not that Bernard Dodd spent all his time in his office. His job took him away at least two days most weeks, not only visiting chaplains, but attending conferences where he met some of those port missionaries, and got an insight into what they were doing. Tough men, some of them, and they needed to be, seeing the sordid, violent side of port life as they did, with the drunkenness and prostitution and the ruining of young lives. They had stories to tell him of girls they had tried to rescue, half dragging them off the ships onto which they were tottering after being made drunk in the convivial atmosphere of the dock-side pubs. But some of those girls had been converted....

Supplying the port missionaries with SGM leaflets and

booklets to suit all classes and races was part of his job, and it brought home to him the realisation that what were sometimes referred to as "the regions beyond" were in fact on our own doorstep.

He was not alone at SGM headquarters in realising it. Roger Kennedy, in his new position as Secretary on the retirement of Norman Brown in 1985, realised it too, and he knew he must do something about it.

12

Team Work

Roger Kennedy was preparing for the meeting held each week in his office for the heads of departments. It was a tight fit to get eight of them into a room that usually had only three chairs, but it was worth it. It helped to strengthen the team spirit among them as they reviewed the past, discussed the present, and planned for the future. He had been in the position of leadership for a couple of years now, but his mind went back to the time when he had joined SGM as its Production Manager, and had embarked on the task of promoting its publications in the UK ...

The decline of Bible knowledge in his own country, and the increasing need for the use of Scripture in evangelism had challenged him. It could no longer be taken for granted that everyone knew basic Christian doctrines, or at least had learned something in Religious Education in schools, even if their parents had never taken them inside a church. As Bernard Dodd was discovering in his contacts with teenagers in the Cadet Corps, a new mission field was emerging right here at home. What has aptly been termed the post-Christian era was producing a generation in the UK as ignorant of the contents of the Bible as the average Muslim or Hindu. It emphasised the necessity laid on every Christian to obey his Master's command to preach the Gospel to everyone – and to start right where he lived.

Roger had realised that his own experience in training

others in the use of SGM Scripture portions in India and the East must be employed in the land of his birth now. He had set about it, with the help of his secretary, by launching a series of weekend conferences for Mission supporters, not only to quicken their interest in the worldwide aspect of the work, but to explain how SGM leaflets and booklets could be used in personal evangelism. They had put on little sketches demonstrating how and how not to present the Scriptures during a conversation, and the "how not to do it" sketches had raised a good deal of laughter; as when a newly married couple setting off on their honeymoon were presented with *Words of Comfort*, or as a young man who had been out of work for months with *It's A Great Life*. But these had helped to get the point across, and then it was easy to give a few practical hints:

"Always have a little supply of SGM titles with you. Half a dozen in a neat folder can be slipped into your pocket or handbag and will take up little room, but you'll have them handy when you need them.

"We've got dozens of publications on various subjects – you can't possibly carry them all with you. Select a few that you can become familiar with, and that will suit the sort of people you meet.

"Perhaps you visit people in hospital. Here is *Day By Day* – a few verses of Scripture for every day of the week, to comfort and encourage. And God speaks through His word. He'll go on speaking, long after you have left. Pray about it, too. Prayer and the Word of God are mighty weapons that can be used by the shyest people, as well as the cheerful extrovert."

Not everyone could use them in the way that Professor Donald Wiseman, Chairman of the SGM Council, used them. His professional duties involved him in a good deal of travelling, and as his wife usually accompanied him they made a point of announcing, by way of the notice board in which ever hotel they happened to be staying, that a short form of divine worship would be held in their room on

Sunday morning. Anyone wishing to attend would be most welcome.

This unusual announcement attracted some surprising visitors, but it did not matter who came, for no denominational note was struck in that simple service. Everyone was handed a booklet. It was entitled *Daily Strength*, and it contained a number of carefully selected Scriptures including the Lord's Prayer, and two or three well-known hymns, it provided all that was needed for the purpose. And, of course, at the end of the service all who had attended were urged to keep their copies of *Daily Strength*.

No, not everyone could do that sort of thing! But even the most inarticulate could enclose *A New Start* in a letter to someone going to college for the first time, or commencing a new job.

SGM supporters were encouraged to use the leaflets not only among English-speaking people. What about those holidays that were spent on the continent? SGM produced Scripture portions in thirty-seven European languages, so why not take some when travelling abroad?

The outcome of Roger's activities to promote SGM at the home base had been the creation of a new department. He lost his secretary in the process, for she was appointed to head it up. She had already been in the Mission nearly thirty years, but before she retired she saw the Extension Department well established, with a young man who knew God had called him into SGM to take her place.

Yes, it had all been very encouraging, reflected Roger, with new doors opening, especially among students, and the new Extension Secretary was enthusiastic. The others were now crammed into his office, and the Extension Secretary was giving his report, 'Things are looking up, especially among students. The Christian Union at Oxford wrote and asked us for 3,500 copies of *Consider Jesus*, sufficient to give to every student going down from University after the exams. We sent them, of course. As a matter of fact, they arrived at a rather significant time.' His voice dropped as he added, 'The time when that girl died of an overdose after a celebration party.'

The case had made headline news in the media, highlighting again the dangers and tragedies of drug taking. The Extension Department had already been talking with representatives of the Universities and Colleges Christian Fellowship about the possibility of SGM producing compilations of Scripture that would be relevant to the problems of the 1980s.

'So it was decided we should produce a series of leaflets entitled *Is There An Alternative To . . .* some of the issues confronting students today – Violence, The Occult, Drugs and Drink, Abortion and Suicide, Wealth and Poverty, Sexual Promiscuity and Perversion. We'd like to have them ready for the next academic year.'

The Production Manager was enthusiastic, too, about the idea of leaflets for young people.'We want to see SGM producing Scriptures which are words from God to a particular situation now,' he said. There had been a big demand for the *When I Am Afraid* leaflet, and it revealed the prevalence of a fear lurking in many minds, ranging from those who were worried about the threat of nuclear warfare to those who were afraid to go out after dark for fear of being mugged. The Chernobyl disaster had added to the general apprehension and the Editorial Secretary, who kept her ear to the ground, commented, 'Many Christians feel that the end times are approaching with famines, disasters, lawlessness and violence all on the increase . . .'

'And earthquake and pestilence,' murmured someone, adding, 'and now AIDS.' There was silence for a moment. Nobody denied that the signs of the times pointed to the need to take every opportunity to spread the Word of God while doors were still open. And the Editorial Secretary, to whose desk came a constant stream of letters and reports of people who had been brought to faith in Christ through reading SGM leaflets and booklets, could cite a number of cases that had come to her recently:

A girl who wrote asking for more booklets because someone had given her one entitled *For Your Need* and it had helped her to give her heart to Jesus.

A man who was thinking of committing suicide who found a copy of *Four Things God Wants You To Know*, on a bus. 'I picked it up and read it and found the solution and comfort for my problems.'

A distressed young widow who was becoming involved in black magic until, when in a train, she was given a copy of *A New Start*, and then turned back to the Lord she had trusted as a child.

A schoolboy who gave his life to Jesus after receiving a copy of *Jesus Will Come Again* at his school Christian Union.

A councillor who, while out canvassing during an election, was given *What Do You Think Of Christ*? and is now worshipping in his local church.

Reports like that were encouraging matter to those who, like the Administrative Secretary, had to deal with mundane matters like computerisation. He was cautiously optimistic about its installation. They had made progress with it, but they hadn't yet got to the stage in the game when everything could be seen at the tap of a key. But there was one thing that had particularly cheered the Production Manager.

'This in-house typesetting is wonderful!' he told them. It was going to solve many of the problems they had been facing with the wide variety of languages in which SGM was asked to produce literature. Commercial firms rarely had the facilities required for typesetting the strange characters, the unusual alignment, the dots and the dashes of foreign languages, and it had been one of the major problems for the Production Manager to find ways of getting the work done.

Then, one day, he went to an exhibition. There he saw the latest system for typesetting, and knew that it could overcome the technical difficulties he was facing. There was only one disadvantage to it. The price was too high. He knew he could not afford to spend £50,000 on that most desirable piece of modern technology. Inwardly disappointed, he was just turning away after making his enquiry when he was told, quite casually, that the WEC Press was already using the system in their work.

WEC Press! Worldwide Evangelization Crusade! There would be no difficulty in approaching them to see if they could help, and no time was lost in doing so. As a result arrangements were made for SGM to acquire "front end" facilities in the shape of a keyboard for computer typesetting. Floppy discs containing the recorded typescript were sent to WEC for processing, then proofs were sent back for the final check before going to the printers for offset printing.

It was revolutionary. The production of literature in out-of-the-way languages, which under the old method would have taken months, could now be speeded up to a matter of days. And with the constantly changing international scene, delays in production could well mean the opportunity for distribution would be lost.

But behind the arrangements that had been made so congenially with WEC was the activity of the God they served. It was typical of the way He so often dealt with them. He did not step in with the spectacular provision for funds or equipment, providing all that they felt they needed, but instead He fitted them in with others who were working for the same end, and serving the same Master. He worked in the context of their circumstances, was with them where they were. The job they had to do was mainly behind the scenes, providing the tools for those in the forefront of evangelism. But He was there with them in the warehouse, in the offices – and in the mundane, everyday task of dealing with modern technology.

Wheels within wheels, fitted together to speed the work – and the Spirit of Life was in the wheels. The visit of the Production Manager to the exhibition would have been fruitless had it not been for the casual remark that provided the extra link with WEC.

'And that is just what we need – contact and co-operation with all Christian organisations,' someone pointed out. 'We need them to ensure that we are producing what is wanted, especially where there is no alternative literature available. And we need them to give the opportunities for wider distribution.'

'We need them for China!' Ronald Young was Area Secretary for the Far East, and he spoke vehemently. The Area Secretary for Africa nodded. 'Nearly a quarter of the world's population is there,' he said, for he knew that there are more people in China than in the whole of Africa and South America combined. And he knew something of the difficulty Ronald Young was having in trying to do something for that country.

'There are great opportunities to help there,' Ronald said. 'But we can't do it ourselves – only in co-operation with those who have specialised knowledge, both for production and distribution. In fact, we can't get on without other organisations. How many of our pioneer editions have been done in co-operation with Wycliffe Bible Translators, for instance?'

Ken Andrewartha, speaking for the Translations Department, replied promptly.

'A good many – Wycliffe is invaluable to our work. And I remember them in their early days in the UK ...' The tape recorder of his memory spun back over thirty years, to the days before the fire, when he was sent to one of their first camps in Chigwell, and got a taste of their pioneer work, living under canvas with some of the men and women who had been or were to be, in the forefront of mission to the unevangelised. That experience was deeply imprinted in his memory.

'And I owe it mainly to A.H. Long,' he said. 'It was Mr Long who had the vision for the British branch of Wycliffe in those early days. He arranged for me to go there. He was Chairman of their Council for years, and the main liaison between us in SGM and Wycliffe. We owe a lot to A.H.L.'

'Not only for his vision.' Ronald Young's memory, too, went back to those days of the 1950s. Of all the staff who had been in the fire he and Ken were the only two now left. Mighell Smith, Joe Carroll, Eric Cook, Winifred Marden, Norman Brown and the others were all on the retirement list. 'Mr Long had insight – he sensed when things were going hard for his staff. I remember a time when I was feeling very frustrated, felt I was being held back from something I wanted to do by the "powers that be". He saw it. He came to the sandwich bar along the road where I went for my lunch, and had a sandwich with me, and said, "You're feeling frustrated, aren't you? Well, just *wait*. Be prepared to wait. If it's of God, nothing can stop it." So I waited. And he was right. It came eventually. But his encouragement at that time meant so much to me as a junior worker. Yes, we owe a lot to A.H.L.'

The reports continued. The alarming increase in postal charges had put a heavy strain on finances, and the Warehouse Manager had been horrified at the cost of the parcels that were going out. But he had been on his toes to find ways and means of saving money, and one triumph had been to send a bulk order to Poland by container instead of by mail. That transaction alone had saved over £1,000.

'You'll have to find inexpensive ways of sending to the Sahara soon,' said Ken cheerfully. 'We've started on the computerised keyboard already. Our first production of a non-roman script will be *Parables Of The Lord Jesus* in Tamajeq. Yes, they'll be getting this booklet at last.'

When the veiled men of the Sahara held these booklets in their hands for the first time, they would have no idea of all that lay behind it – the years of unseen translation work by missionaries who had painstakingly learned their language, committed it to writing, checked with translators who had pored over books, checked back again, questioning the literal meaning of this word and that word to ensure that it was correct. The file marked Tamajeq in the SGM Translation Department would reveal only a little of it.

The file marked Dari would uncover another story, recorded so tersely that it only supplied the bare bones of what SGM saw as the hand of God working in history. After years of starting, then stopping, the production in the Dari language had been written, checked, re-checked and eventually printed. They could be read and understood by millions of the people of Afghanistan, if only they could reach them. But there seemed no possibility of that happening now. The hold of Islam had tightened in the country, and Christian witness was being throttled.

Then came the invasion of Soviet troops, and the wholesale evacuation of hundreds of thousands of Afghans into neighbouring Pakistan. These refugees crossed the borders in larger and smaller groups, arriving in a land where there was no restriction on the distribution of those Scriptures. Christian workers going in and out of the refugee camps could distribute them freely, and the Afghans could receive them fearlessly, and read for the first time, in their own language, the Good News of salvation.

'Opportunity seems to me rather like a revolving door,' said Roger. 'The door swings round and round, sometimes so full you can't get in. And when there is an opening, you must be ready to get in quickly, before it swings on and you're left waiting.'

The revolving door of opportunity, swinging round, swinging past, swinging away. One hundred years ago a printer in Birmingham, William Walters, had seen it and entered, and had started something that today was far more widespread than anything he had envisaged. Down through the changing decades, through two world wars, into the new era of nuclear power and advanced technology, doors of opportunity for the dissemination of the Word of God had been swinging round, swinging past, swinging away. Nothing remained static, and the opportunity could be missed through inattention, or hesitant deliberation, or inadequate resources.

And the opportunity was not only to reach to the ends of the earth through radio, through cassettes, through the time-honoured methods of literature brought up to date. The opportunity was right here, in our own country, with its hundred and more ethnic minority groups, refugees from Vietnam, immigrants from Bangladesh, students from the Third World, tourists from the Middle East. And the man in the street.

Day after day the mail brought letters from countries all round the world asking SGM for some of their literature in hundreds of languages, and in the mail was a constant little stream of testimonies about people who had been brought in touch with the living Christ through what they had read. A woman in Fiji, a Muslim from Pakistan, a schoolboy, a woman dying of cancer...

The Spirit of Life was in those revolving doors of opportunity, with a country closed to the Gospel suddenly opening... another closing... refugees flooding over borders, immigrants clamouring for entrance into the affluent countries of the West, remote tribal groups responding to the Gospel and urgent requests coming for something for them to read, prison chaplains telling of unprecedented responsiveness, missionaries in the inner cities looking for something simple enough and relevant enough to arrest bewildered minds there...

Roger looked round on the group squeezed into his office with subdued excitement. "Back room boys" they sometimes called themselves laughingly, but they knew that they were producing something that those in the frontline of evangelism needed. 'We would be like soldiers in the firing line without any ammunition if you didn't let us have your literature,' they were sometimes told. The opportunities opening before them seemed almost more than they could grasp, and demands greater than they could respond to.

There was a sense of quiet urgency in the room now, as each faced the tasks that lay before them, from Ken in the Translations Department to the Warehouse Manager wondering how he would get all the orders dealt with when there weren't enough packers to do the job.

Then, as so often happened, silence fell. And just as the men and women who had been their predecessors had been aware, time and time again, they were conscious of God's presence. The presence of the Lord who had been there in the years before the fire, He who had brought His workers through it then, He who was with each of His workers now, ready to answer when they turned to Him for help.

The One who was really in control.

'MY SPIRIT REMAINS AMONG YOU. DO NOT FEAR.'

Roger drew a little breath, then looked round and said quietly, 'Let's pray...'

TO THE HEART OF THE CITY

Phyllis Thompson

Founded to take the Gospel to the dark, inhospitable corners of the city, the London City Mission has now completed 150 years of work among the urban poor. The story of the missionaries' patient visits to sometimes unfriendly homes, persistent help to those in need, and unwavering proclamation of the Christian truth they knew could change lives, is told here in Phyllis Thompson's lively style. A fascinating record, its material is drawn from the personal experiences of the missionaries as they went to police stations and schools, talked to cabbies and bus drivers, visited prisons and hospitals.

The needs of the city have changed but spiritual hunger is unabated; one hundred missionaries continue the work of the LCM today.

'I recommend this book wholeheartedly. It is both exciting and challenging. It cannot fail to thrill and inspire any reader.' Michael Green, *Church Times*

'This book is full of stories and is required reading for all who work in urban areas.' *Baptist Times*

MADAME GUYON – MARTYR OF THE HOLY SPIRIT

Phyllis Thompson

The story of Jeanne de la Mothe Guyon is a remarkable one. An apparently ordinary wife and mother living in seventeenth-century France, her deep love for God and her unswerving Christian commitment stirred up hatred and opposition in the highest political and eccelsiastical circles of her time. The spread of her simple teaching on the love of God, the abandonment of self-centredness and the acceptance of God's will brought Madame Guyon imprisonment and interrogation, but she remained devoted to her Saviour to the end.

'To write her story has been a fascinating task,' says Phyllis Thompson. 'Relevant, instructive and challenging, the message she proclaimed does not alter with the times.'

'**Most readable and inspiring**' CLC *Floodtide*

'**Challenging reading**' *Christian Weekly Newspapers*